BABY
SIGN LANGUAGE

KNACK

BABY
SIGN LANGUAGE

A Step-by-Step Guide to Communicating with Your Little One

SUZIE CHAFIN

Photographs by Johnston Bell Grindstaff

Technical review by Anne E. Pidano, Ph.D.

Guilford, Connecticut
An imprint of Globe Pequot Press

Copyright © 2010 by Morris Book Publishing, LLC

ALL RIGHTS RESERVED. No part of this book may be reproduced or transmitted in any form by any means, electronic or mechanical, including photocopying and recording, or by any information storage and retrieval system, except as may be expressly permitted in writing from the publisher. Requests for permission should be addressed to Globe Pequot Press, Attn: Rights and Permissions Department, P.O. Box 480, Guilford, CT 06437.

Knack is a registered trademark of Morris Publishing Group, LLC, and is used with express permission.

Editor-in-Chief: Maureen Graney
Editor: Imee Curiel
Cover Design: Paul Beatrice, Bret Kerr
Text Design: Paul Beatrice
Layout: Joanna Beyer
Cover and interior photos by Johnston Bell Grindstaff

Library of Congress Cataloging-in-Publication Data

Chafin, Suzie.
  Knack baby sign language : a step-by-step guide to communicating with your little one / Suzie Chafin ; photographs by Johnston Grindstaff ; technical review by Anne E. Pidano.
     p. cm.
  Includes index.
  ISBN 978-1-59921-614-0
  1. Nonverbal communication in infants—Study and teaching.
  2. Interpersonal communication in infants—Study and teaching.
  3. American Sign Language—Study and teaching. I. Title.
  BF720.C65C43 2010
  419'.1—dc22
                        2009029672

The following manufacturers/names appearing in *Knack Baby Sign Language* are trademarks: Band-Aid®, Barbie™, Plexiglas®, Velcro®

The information in this book is true and complete to the best of our knowledge. All recommendations are made without guarantee on the part of the author or Globe Pequot Press. The author and Globe Pequot Press disclaim any liability in connection with the use of this information.

Printed in China
10 9 8 7 6 5 4 3 2 1

Author Dedication

For Sam, Lauren, Jon, and James, who showed me signing with babies is possible. For Andy, who helped me teach them.

—S.C.

Author Acknowledgments

I am deeply indebted to several people who made this work possible. First, my thanks and gratitude to Maureen Graney for giving me the opportunity to write this book and for her support, encouragement, and contributions. Thank you, Imee Curiel, for your direction, insight, and support. John Grindstaff's photographs and artistic influence provide the visual backbone for this book. Thank you, John, for your fabulous work. Barb Doyen, once again thank you for your support, representation, and constant words of encouragement. Last, thank you to my family for the sacrifices you each made so I could work on this book.

—S.C.

Photographer Dedication

To my mother, Dorothea Grindstaff, for your love and for believing in me.

—J.G.

Photographer Acknowledgments

Thanks to the publishing team at Globe Pequot Press, especially Maureen Graney, Imee Curiel, and Katie Benoit, for giving me an opportunity to do the photography for this unique book. And to author Suzie Chafin for her gifted writing to reveal beautiful words. Also thanks to the beautiful and handsome models— Tilde Edington, Tindra Edington, Barry Elliott, Laine Elliott-Mendelsohn, Zora Elliott-Mendelsohn, Hanna Johnston-Shaw, Camela Klusza, Leia Klusza, Joshua Mendelsohn, Grace Nathanson, Dov Nathanson, Zeke Ortiz, and Zion Ortiz—for their time and help with ideas in the art of ASL. Special thanks to the parents of the child models for their time and willingness to work with me. Thanks to my wife, Natalie, for her boundless help as a sign master, assistant, and much more. Thanks to my children, Jarvis, Raquel, and Jake, for their support.

—J.G.

CONTENTS

INTRODUCTION

So you want to teach your child sign language? You've just taken the first step to making that goal a reality. You may be wondering, "Can it really be done? Is it really possible to teach my little baby to talk using sign language?" Unequivocally yes.

All four of my children used sign language during the first two years of their lives (and beyond). My oldest, with whom I had the most time to spend working, picked up a large vocabulary and used signs often. Because he had chronic ear infections, signing was especially helpful for him. He could easily communicate with me when his ear was hurting, or when he was hungry, and tell me what he wanted, all just using his hands. When his little sister was born just 21 months after him, he helped teach the signs to her. Several years later came our identical twin boys, who also signed. By then, time was a precious commodity. Even with four kids five years of age and younger, we were still able to teach sign language and found it to be a very useful and effective communication tool. Though our twins didn't have the signing vocabulary that our oldest had, using a core group of signs made my life easier and simpler.

Today, though those baby twins are now nine years old, sign language still peppers our everyday conversations. The *I love you* sign is used often, through car windows, and at bedtime just before we close the door. Even just walking through the room, we often raise our hands, saying, "I love you," and our kids are reminded by that simple gesture that we love them. My oldest, now a 14-year-old milk addict, still asks for milk by flashing me the milk sign. While eating, if the kids' mouths are full they still ask

for more using their hands. On a recent vacation we were able to communicate across ski lift lines with simple commands like *wait* and *stop*. So, does sign language have a benefit beyond the baby years? Absolutely!

The Benefits of Sign Language

If you are interested in achieving effective communication with your child, positioning your child for greater classroom success later, and having a less frustrated and more content child, teaching sign is well worth the effort.

1. Increased Communication

Imagine being able to understand, talk, and communicate easily and effectively with your six month old. Who wouldn't want that ability, right? Sign language makes this possible. As early as the age of six months, your baby is able to begin repeating, understanding, and using sign language to tell you what he wants or needs.

Effective give-and-take verbal communication usually does not occur until your child is around 18 months old, which means using sign language can potentially allow you to understand and communicate a full year earlier. You won't have to wonder if a cry means your baby is hungry, tired, or wants a favorite blanket or pacifier. Instead, through sign, baby will tell you, eliminating the crying guessing game. Not only will you understand baby earlier, but you and baby will experience less frustration and fewer tears, and the moments that you spend together will be more fulfilling without the aggravation of misunderstandings.

2. Reduced Frustration

Deciphering tears is never easy. Hungry? Tired? Does she want a toy, a cracker, to go outside? Before articulation of words is possible, your child has long understood the meaning of food, drink, mom, dad, and favorite possessions. Yet the ability to articulate the words has not caught up with your child's conceptual understanding. Through sign, your child will be able to say words though his verbal skills are not yet acquired. Equipping your child with a vocabulary of signs to communicate feelings, ideas, and desires can help reduce frustration caused by being unable to communicate otherwise. When you as a parent understand your baby and can give him what he wants or needs, you will feel more relaxed and will experience less stress in your parenting.

3. Increased Bonding

Sign language creates another bonding opportunity for you and your child. When signing is used properly in an encouraging environment, the increased communication and understanding can weave your family unit closer together.

4. Increased Language and Verbal Acquisition Skills

Most people don't understand how using signs can actually help your child gain language and verbal usage earlier. Because your child will be learning the conceptual meanings of words through sign, your child is understanding language at an earlier age. Research indicates that gesturing or the use of baby sign can be an effective and important tool in your child's language development.

A 2009 study by Elizabeth Crais, Linda Watson, and Grace Baranek at the University of North Carolina found a "strong relationship between gesture use and later communicative skills" and a 2005 report by Jana Iverson and Susan Goldin-Meadow suggests that the use of gesturing might pave the way for language development. The report stated, "The fact that gesture allows children to communicate meanings that they may have difficulty expressing verbally raises the possibility that gesture serves a facilitating function for language learning." The report even went so far as to say, "There is evidence that the act of gesturing can itself promote learning."

Additionally, your child will have more practice communicating, which helps with classroom adjustment later. In fact, children who use sign language as babies have been shown to have a higher IQ than children who do not sign as babies. A study performed by Linda Acredolo and Susan Goodwyn in 2000 found a 12-point I.Q. advantage in children who used baby signs during their second year of life over children who had no exposure to gesturing or baby sign.

Frequently Asked Questions

You might wonder, "Will this baby sign language concept really work?" It is normal and healthy to have a little skepticism. Here are some common questions and concerns parents considering signing may have:

How much time will it take?

The answer to this question depends on how much you want to integrate sign language into your family dynamic. If you choose just to season your communication with a few sign essentials, then teaching sign language won't take long at all. Demonstrating and encouraging your child to learn and use a few signs will probably happen very quickly if you use the signs in context and consistently. If you choose to develop a large vocabulary, then begin small and add on as your child masters the words. Learning more words will obviously take more time. Use what is best for your family. If you have older children, teach them at the same time, taking advantage of the opportunity to teach a foreign language.

What does it require of me?

Don't worry; knowing sign language already is not a prerequisite. In this book you will find the tools to easily learn and teach your child sign language. If your fingers feel off at first, that's okay. Remember, you are learning a new language too, so it's okay to feel awkward and to make mistakes.

While experience is not needed, a consistent effort on your part is. Using the signs consistently, in context, every day will ensure signing success.

It will also require patience. Learning sign language does not often occur overnight. Don't get frustrated and don't give up if you don't see immediate success.

You will also need to add a little more time to your daily routine. It may take just a little longer to eat, get dressed, or get bedtime going when you first start to incorporate signing into your routine. But in the long run, knowing and using those signs will make those activities run more efficiently.

Signing requires commitment. If you are only semi-committed or use the signs sporadically, then you probably won't see much benefit. Partner your signing with reading aloud and lots of talking to help get the most out of the experience.

Do I have enough time?

Think you don't have enough time? That is the beauty of sign language. It is a supplementary tool to help you as a parent increase communication. So supplement as you are able with the words you find most helpful. For us, mealtime signs were the most used. Next, animal signs were fun to learn, and we found clothing signs helpful in getting dressed. No two families will need to use the ex-

act same signs. Pick and choose what works best for your family and your family dynamics. As you go through each chapter, don't feel compelled to learn every single sign. Decide which will best aid and assist communication in your home, and learn those signs.

How to Use This Book

Are you ready to begin effective communication with your baby? The first six chapters focus on signs that you can easily teach your child up to age 12 months. It's probably best to wait to begin introducing sign to your baby until he is at least six months old. (Introducing sign before this age certainly won't harm your child, but it will be more for your benefit and practice than for your child.) We'll begin using mealtime signs, which are easy to introduce in context as your child eats. Chapters 7 through 12 focus on signs that can enlarge and enrich your vocabulary foundation. These signs may be a little more complex and require more refined fine motor development, and are geared for the older baby. Last, chapters 13 through 17 include signs for all ages, including many that you may find appropriate for preschool-aged children. Chapters 18 and 19 show the American Manual Alphabet and numbers. Go ahead and familiarize yourself with the American Manual Alphabet. Many of the other everyday signs you learn will be based on the letters of the alphabet, so knowing these letter signs will help you as you acquire each new sign.

Chapter 20 provides fun finger play songs ranging from simple to longer and more complex songs. Explore these songs for some creative movement fun and to encourage expression through sign. There is also a resource directory including helpful Web sites.

Flex those fingers and get ready to communicate with your baby!

TOP TEN DOS AND DON'TS

Remember, using sign language with your baby is all about increasing communication and reducing frustration. To encourage success, keep the following principles in mind.

Top Ten Things to Do When Signing with Your Baby:

1. **Be consistent.** Use the signs throughout the day consistently and in the same context.

2. **Do it often.** It is not enough to show your child a sign one day, or even to use it for a week. Your child needs to see the signs often, at home and out and about.

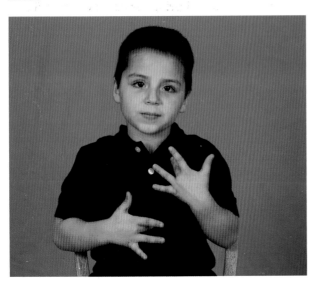

3. **Use a few signs at once.** Introducing a few signs at the same time in context is good. Introducing many signs out of context will leave your child overwhelmed.

4. **Do it with the goal in mind—communication.** Teaching your child sign language is about communication, not about teaching your child a trick or impressing others.

5. **Read, read, read.** Reading aloud helps increase verbal and language acquisition skills. Read to your child often and sign as you read.

6. **Help child with signs.** Your child will need your help. Gently help him form the signs, then repeat the sign back to him.

7. **Wait for mastery** with signs you have already introduced before introducing more new signs.

8. **Look for opportunities.** Teachable moments are all around you. Sign and talk to your baby about the world around him.

9. **Do it everywhere with everyone.** Sign language is not just for home use. Be consistent by using it everywhere at all times.

10. **Be supportive and encouraging.** Learning sign language should be a positive experience.

Top Ten Things Not to Do When Signing with Your Baby:

1. **Don't demand signing or withhold objects if child refuses to sign.** Don't frustrate your child by forcing him to sign. Signing should reduce, not increase frustration.

2. **Don't turn signing into a negative experience.** If your child just isn't getting it, that's okay. In time the signs will come. Don't express negativity.

3. **Don't create tears instead of reduce tears** by overwhelming child with too many signs or by being demanding.

4. **Don't be sporadic.** Success with signing will only come with consistent use of signs.

5. **Don't overwhelm your child** by going too fast, using too many signs, or by using signs out of context.

6. **Don't make your child show off her skills.** Your child is not a dog who has graduated from obedience school. Signing is for communication, not for tricks.

7. **Don't put too much pressure on yourself.** Success is subjective. Use sign so it works for, not against, your family.

8. **Don't give up easily.** Remember, signing takes time. You'll have to invest a little time before you may see the reward.

9. **Don't have unrealistic expectations.** If your child is three or four months old, don't expect to see results yet. Don't expect to introduce a sign once and have your child sign back to you. Go into teaching sign with realistic expectations.

10. **Don't introduce signs without tone, inflection, and excitement.** Pique interest with animation and excitement. A boring tone and lack of excitement will not entice your child to sign.

TIME TO EAT

Mealtime is a great opportunity to use, introduce, and teach signs to baby

Congratulate yourself for taking the time and effort to increase communication with your child. Learning and teaching sign language can help alleviate frustration and stress for both you and your child. Ready to get started?

We will begin with learning American Sign Language signs at mealtime. Why mealtime? It is the most natural and easiest place to integrate signs into the daily routine. Baby is in a high chair or booster seat, which not only makes using both of your hands easier, but it provides a location for baby to be a captive audience.

You will learn the words: *hungry, all done, more*, and *eat*. These four signs are perfect for getting started and seeing

KNACK BABY SIGN LANGUAGE

Hungry

- Form the letter C shape. (Refer to the American Manual Alphabet in Chapter 18.)

- Place the letter C at the top of your chest with fingertips touching your chest.

- Move the C downward on your chest toward the top of your tummy.

All Done or Finished

- Use this sign after your baby has clearly indicated she is finished eating or playing with a certain object. Later, she may use this sign even in a social setting when she has had enough.

- Place both hands about shoulder level with palms open and facing forward.

- Swivel the hands back and forth several times.

- Say, "All done" or "Finished" as you make this sign.

how easily sign language can be integrated into your routine. Don't begin with too many signs at once. Using these first four signs will begin to make you comfortable and confident in your ability to sign and teach your child. Use these signs often, every time you eat or drink with your child. Speak the words as you introduce the signs and use the signs in context. Next, help your child sign the word after you have signed it.

ZOOM

Repetition and consistency are essential for success. Model for your child with words and signs. For example, if you are working on integrating *more*, model this way: "Do you want more cereal? More?" while signing and speaking the word repeatedly. Then give her more. Next, help baby sign *more* by gently moving her hands for her. Keep doing this with every meal.

More

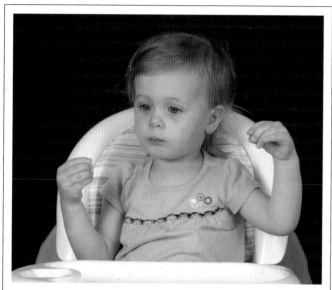

- *More* uses both hands. Each hand closes the tips of the fingers to the tip of the thumb.

- Bring the hands to meet and pull them apart again.

- Make sure that every time you say the word *more*, you're signing it at the same time.

- Repetition is essential for quick learning. Not only does repeating help the baby learn the sign, it also provides great modeling for the baby's future verbal skills.

Eat

- *Eat* uses the dominant hand. If you are right handed, use your right hand.

- Bring the thumb to meet your fingertips.

- In a back-and-forth motion, move your hand to and away from your mouth.

- This motion imitates the act of eating something.

WHAT I WANT

Understanding what your child wants reduces frustration for you and your child

Teaching your child how to sign will give her a voice for some simple concepts and words that she is not yet able to articulate. Instead of crying and screaming for a bottle or for a drink, she will be able to quickly, quietly, and easily tell you exactly what she wants. Certainly tears, pointing, and grunting communicate some needs and wants, but pointing is not specific, and frustration usually mounts as baby and parent grapple to understand one another. Through the use of the hands you are giving your baby the ability to talk to you before she is able to do so verbally.

It may sound counterintuitive to teach a hearing baby to talk with her hands. Shouldn't parents be more concerned with

Bottle

Note that here the sign is being made with the palm down. Young children may create their own variations on the standard hand movements.

Drink

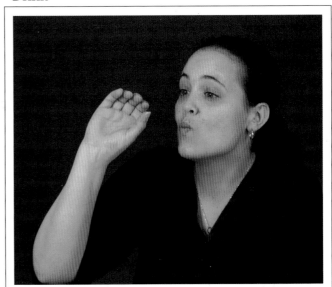

- *Bottle* uses both hands. Place your stationary hand in a flat, horizontal position with the palm up.

- With your dominant hand, form the letter C (refer to the American Manual Alphabet in Chapter 18) and turn it horizontally so the thumb faces up. Place the dominant hand on the stationary hand.

- Move the dominant hand upward, and constrict the C into the letter O, representing the tighter closed end of the bottle.

- Form the letter C with the dominant hand. (Refer to the American Manual Alphabet in Chapter 18.)

- Begin the sign at about chest level.

- Move the letter C to your lips as though your hand is holding a cup or glass.

- Tip the C as though you were taking a drink from the glass.

teaching their babies to talk? But by signing you are actually laying a strong foundation for verbal language acquisition. And there is no evidence that learning sign language delays normal speech development. In fact, research shows that learning sign may actually enhance future language skills (Iverson and Goldwin-Meadow). Additionally, children who sign as babies and toddlers tend to read at an earlier age.

The four signs that are introduced in this spread—*bottle, drink, milk,* and *want*—communicate basic concepts that are a part of baby's everyday world. In addition, they are simple

enough that even infants as young as six months old can begin to form these words and begin to communicate through their hands. If your child isn't able to form the exact hand movements yet, that's okay! Early signers will often make their own variation of the sign, or will just do part of the sign.

Milk

- *Milk* uses the dominant hand.
- *Milk* emulates the motion of milking a cow.
- Move your hand in and out of a tight fist several times.
- Make sure to say "Milk" as you use this sign. Use this sign consistently and often. It is one of the easiest for babies to form and to learn quickly.

Want

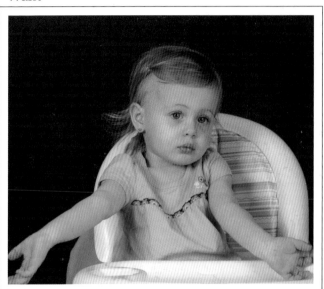

- *Want* uses both hands.
- Begin with both hands at about chest level, slightly extended. Have palms facing upwards with the fingers slightly bent.
- Bring both hands simultaneously towards your body as you slightly bend your fingers in a gripping motion.
- Facial expression and tone of voice should be married to the sign. Be sure to look and sound as though you want something.

IN THE HIGH CHAIR
Learning signs every child will need and use in the high chair

The high chair or booster seat is destined to become a place your baby will know well. Not only is it the place where she gets her favorite snacks, meals, and drinks, but it will also be the place where she learns how to talk to you. Here we will learn the signs *bib*, *spoon*, *cup*, and *bowl*. So, what if you aren't using a bowl or cup yet? That's okay; just don't teach those signs yet. Wait to introduce those signs when it is appropriate. Signs should always be introduced in context, so there is no point in teaching *cup* if your child is still using a bottle. You decide what words you want to teach. You can always come back to words that you want to acquire later. Begin with integrating just one or two signs into your routine. Once you and your child have mastered those two signs, go ahead and add one or two more. Adding too many signs

Bib

- *Bib* uses both hands.

- Pretend to place a bib on yourself with fingers clasped as though you are holding the bib.

- Next, pull the hands behind your neck as though to fasten the bib.

- Remember to always verbally speak the word as you sign the word.

Spoon

- Form the letter U with the dominant hand, using both the index and middle finger extended while all other fingers are closed. (Refer to the American Manual Alphabet in Chapter 18.)

- Scoop the letter U upwards in the way you would use a spoon.

- Say the word "Spoon" as you sign it.

too quickly will hinder understanding and may frustrate both you and your child.

Teaching signs in the high chair might seem like an extra chore at a time of day that can already be stressful. Realize that signing is worth the time and effort you put into it. As your child begins to understand these important words and concepts you'll see the value and benefit of your effort.

ZOOM
Most infants begin to babble and form beginning words between 9 and 12 months. However, effective verbal communication usually does not take place until around 18 months to two years. Through the use of sign, you can potentially begin to have effective communication with your baby as early as six months old.

The signs for bowl and cup are iconic signs, meaning they look like the word being signed.

Cup

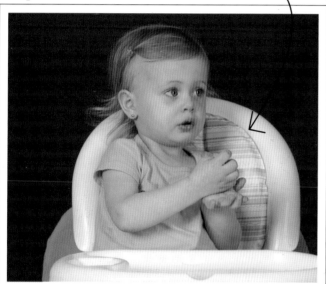

- *Cup* looks very similar to the sign for bottle. Begin by forming the letter C with your dominant hand.

- Hold the stationary hand flat, horizontal with the palm facing upwards.

- Place the letter C on the stationary hand and move the hand upwards. Your hand will look as though it is holding a cup or a glass.

Bowl

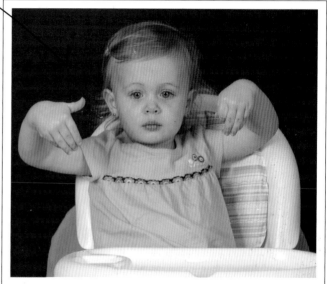

- *Bowl* uses both hands. Begin with the hands side by side. Cup the hands slightly, and face palms upward.

- Simultaneously move each hand outward in an arc as though it were forming the shape of the bowl.

- Make sure you wait to sign when your child is looking at you. Repeat the sign as you say the word to help gain association between the object, the word, and the sign.

5

FINGER FOODS
Use snacks and meals to expand your signing vocabulary

At around six months old, most babies have been given the go-ahead from their doctors for the introduction of solid foods. Signs of readiness include being able to sit well when supported and being able to swallow food. As you are introducing solids, you'll probably be using these words quite a bit at mealtime: *banana*, *apple*, *cookie*, and *cracker*. These common words have simple signs that you and baby can easily learn. Remember to model both with your hands and with your voice as you show and introduce a new sign. Don't forget to continue using the signs you have already taught your child.

While you are in the process of establishing the habit of signing during meals, go ahead and establish habits that will create healthy living and eating. Have all meals at the highchair

Banana

- *Banana* is a fun two-handed sign.

- Before you begin, imagine peeling a banana. Your hands will be mimicking that motion.

- With your stationary hand, form the number 1 with your index finger extended.

- With your dominant hand, pretend you are peeling back the skin from a banana.

- Baby will quickly understand and associate the sign for banana with the word for banana.

Apple

Our model found it easier to use her index finger rather than her thumb. Remember, technical accuracy is not as important as communication.

- *Apple* uses only one hand.

- Using your dominant hand, form the letter A with the thumb beside the folded-down fingers. (Refer to the American Manual Alphabet in Chapter 18.)

- Place the thumb of the letter A on the side of your chin.

- Slightly turn your wrist back and forth.

or in your lap at a table. From an early age, ensure television is not part of mealtime. Provide a balanced diet and resist the temptation to introduce sweets or fast food. Last, stop feeding when baby is full, not when the jar or bowl is empty. Set a good foundation for mealtime habits later on in life.

ZOOM

The guidelines for introducing solid foods are similar to the guidelines for introducing new signs. Timing and an awareness of baby's mood can mean the difference between success and frustration. Don't force baby to sign or try something new when he's fussy or tired. And introduce new foods one at a time.

Cookie

- *Cookie* uses both hands.

- Hold the stationary hand flat, palm facing upward.

- Use the dominant hand to form a C with the fingertips placed on top of the stationary hand.

- Move the C back and forth as though you are using a cookie cutter.

Cracker

- *Cracker* uses both arms and hands.

- Begin with the stationary arm bent with the elbow pointing forward.

- Form a fist with the dominant hand.

- Place the dominant fist on the elbow. Next, move it away from the elbow.

- Repeat this movement, much like knocking on a door, several times.

HOW I WANT IT
Descriptive words form a natural progression in baby's ability to communicate her needs

Here you will learn signs that will help your child describe what she is experiencing. You will teach your child to say *hot*, *cold*, *big*, and *little*. Understanding these concepts is part of your baby's growing comprehension of the world around her.

As you observe your child learning and properly using

various signs, take a moment to make sure she is on track in other areas as well. It is always a good idea to check that your child is close to, meeting, or exceeding key developmental milestones. If your child was born full term and is not yet meeting these milestones, it is important to talk to your doctor to determine why.

Hot

- *Hot* uses only one hand.

- Form a loose, somewhat open C with your dominant hand.

- Begin the sign with the loose C close to your mouth, fingertips toward your mouth.

- Rotate and move downward the C so that it ends with the fingertips facing away from your body.

Cold

- *Cold* uses both arms and hands.

- Envision yourself freezing and shivering, and the natural movement you make when you are shivering.

- Tuck your arms close beside your body, fists tight and moving back and forth.

- As you say "Cold," be sure your face is saying it, too!

6- to 7-month-old milestone check

Physically, it is appropriate for your child to be doing the following:

Be able to lift head while placed on stomach.

Be able to sit up in a high chair.

When held in a standing position, be able to bear almost all of her own weight on her legs.

Be able to roll over from back to stomach.

Be able to rake or pick up a small object.

Be able to sit, even for just a moment, with little assistance.

Cognitively, it is appropriate for your child to be doing the following:

Begin to imitate actions such as blowing lips, smiling, or sticking out the tongue.

May begin to fear strangers.

Begin to make sounds resembling short words.

Be able to know and recognize mom and dad.

Big

- *Big* uses both hands.

- Place both hands at about chest level, palms facing each other.

- Depending on how "big" something is will determine how far apart your hands are. If something is large, place hands about shoulder level apart.

- If describing something enormous, then have fun being creative. Use voice, facial expression, and placing hands very far apart to convey the message of something very large.

Little

- *Little* uses both hands.

- Begin with both palms spread apart at chest level, with the palms of each hand facing each other.

- Next, move both hands together to signify something growing smaller.

- Say the word "Little" with inflection as you sign, helping to convey the meaning of something small or little.

9

SIMPLE COMMANDS

Be able to instruct your child or ask a question with simple signs

The next four signs, *wait*, *full*, *stop*, and *enough*, can be used in a variety of settings. Begin using these signs at mealtime to signal when baby is done eating, or when pouring milk or cereal, or even to ask for patience. Once your child has a clear understanding of what these words mean, go ahead and use them whenever and wherever appropriate, indoors or outdoors.

These signs are especially useful as basic commands to keep your child safe. In just a few short months, your pre-crawling or crawling baby is going to be very mobile, making safety more of an issue. Taking the time to ready your house now can help prevent catastrophic accidents later.

If your child is showing signs of emerging mobility, it's a good idea to head to the hardware store. Electrical outlet plugs will

Wait

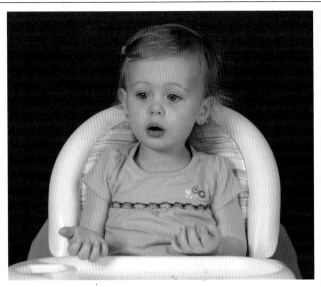

- *Wait* uses both hands. Hold both hands at about chest level.

- The palms of both hands face your body.

- Wiggle the fingers of the hands back and forth.

- As you say the word "Wait," use a tone that conveys the meaning too.

Full

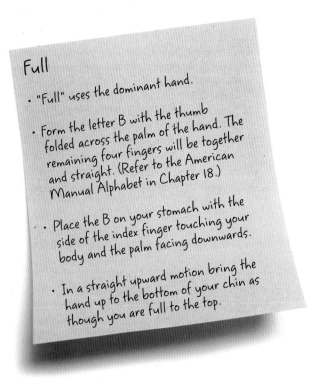

- "Full" uses the dominant hand.

- Form the letter B with the thumb folded across the palm of the hand. The remaining four fingers will be together and straight. (Refer to the American Manual Alphabet in Chapter 18.)

- Place the B on your stomach with the side of the index finger touching your body and the palm facing downwards.

- In a straight upward motion bring the hand up to the bottom of your chin as though you are full to the top.

help keep your child safe from accidental electrocution. Keep cords away from baby's reach to prevent unwanted objects from falling onto baby. Ensure that stairs are blocked by safety gates. If you are in an older home, check the distance between railings. If the distance between each rail is greater than 4 inches, then it is necessary to cover the railing with Plexiglas or other protective covering. Buy and install latches for all drawers, cabinets, and cupboards that contain dangerous items such as cleaning agents and medicines and keep them out of baby's reach.

Notice how the stationary hand is palm down, instead of palm up. It's okay if your child alters or changes the sign for ease of communication.

Stop

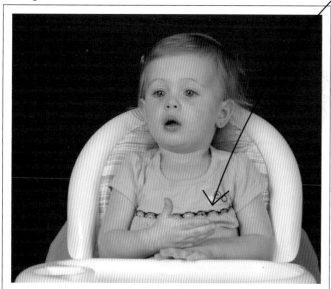

- *Stop* uses both hands.

- Hold the stationary hand in a number 5 position, flat, palm facing upwards. (Refer to the number list in Chapter 19.)

- With the dominant hand, form a flat, closed palm with thumb out and the rest of the fingers touching.

- Strike the dominant hand against the stationary hand abruptly and with force, as though something should stop immediately.

Enough

- *Enough* uses both hands. Form a closed fist with the stationary hand.

- Form a flat palm with the dominant hand.

- Brush the dominant hand over the stationary hand two times.

- Use this sign at mealtime, story time, bath time, and more!

YOU & ME
Teach baby easy signs and help him bond with the important people in his life

Signing gives you purposeful communication. The time spent is intentional and makes use of the teachable moments. It is a great way for parents and grandparents to bond with baby. Try to encourage family members and child-care providers to use signs too. They don't have to learn everything you know, but teach them the ones your child uses the most. They can also reap the benefit of reduced frustration and will enjoy this fun way to bond with your child.

Here we will learn the signs *mom*, *dad*, *baby*, and *love*. Use these signs as mom or dad comes through the door, or when mom or dad is outside in the yard or in the other room. Help encourage association by saying and signing the words

Mom

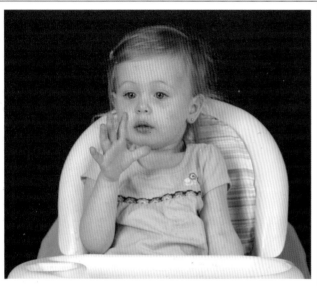

- *Mom* uses one hand only.

- Make the number 5 with your dominant hand. (Refer to the number list in Chapter 19.)

- Place the thumb on the chin.

- Move the hand just slightly back and forth on and off the chin.

Dad

- *Dad* uses one hand only.

- *Dad* is very similar to *mom* except that it is made on the forehead.

- Sign the number 5 with the thumb in the middle of the forehead.

- Move the thumb on and off the forehead repeatedly.

- Your child may not always perform the sign exactly; placement of the hands might be slightly off. Don't worry if the sign isn't exactly right. What is important is that your child is using the gesture and trying to communicate with you.

often. The more you repeat, and model through speaking and signing, the more success you will have. It's not enough to work on it for one day or even one week. Signing requires effort every day, throughout the day. Help baby say the signs back to you by gently moving her hands as you say the words out loud. When dad comes home after work, make a production, be excited, and verbally talk about daddy coming home, coupled with the sign *dad* at the same time.

ZOOM

Here are other ways to bond with your baby: *Touch/Massage*. Babies thrive on being touched. Try giving baby a soothing massage after bath time. *Singing*. Thankfully, babies aren't *American Idol* judges. They don't care how off-tune and out of beat you may be. The sound of your voice is soothing to your child.

Baby

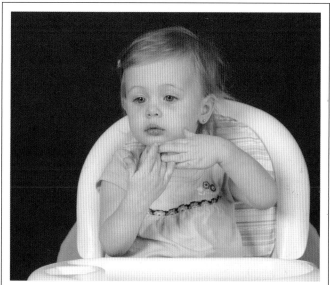

- *Baby* uses both hands and arms.

- Cradle both arms together as though you are holding a baby.

- Rock your arms back and forth as though you are rocking a baby.

- Have a sweet expression on your face as though you are looking at a tiny baby.

Love

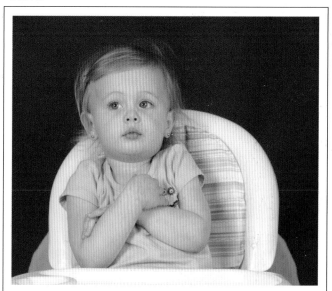

- *Love* uses both arms.

- Cross one arm over the other arm, forming a large X shape on your chest.

- Keep the fists closed and tight.

- To say *rest*, you would use this same sign, but instead of closed fists your hands would be flat.

TUMMY TIME

It's never too early (or too late) to begin incorporating sign into your daily routine

Here we will learn four signs: *up*, *down*, *back*, and *tummy*. Consider how often these simple words are said—in the car, at mealtime, playtime, and more. Take advantage of every opportunity to sign as you speak. You'll find that signing with your child is not so difficult to integrate into your daily routine. Watching your child speak back to you with her hands will encourage you to try new signs and increase her vocabulary even more. You can choose to use as much or as little signing as you feel is appropriate. The important thing is that it is helping you and your child communicate.

For a while, you might feel silly making all these signs to a baby who seems to be nonresponsive. You might even feel

Up

- *Up* uses both hands.

- Cup both hands as though you are lifting something.

- Another way you can sign *up* is by simply pointing upwards with your dominant hand and index finger.

- Remember, signing success comes with repetition and consistent use.

Down

- Like the motion for *up*, cup both hands as though you are holding something.

- Next, move both hands in a downward motion, as though you are placing something down.

- Don't get frustrated if you don't have immediate success. Continue to sign, and before too long your child will be signing too!

like you are performing to a disinterested audience. Don't get discouraged. While it is never too late (or too early!) to begin signing with your baby or child, it is best to begin signing around the age of six months old. Babies are typically ready to begin using their hands to sign back to you between six and nine months old. As a parent, you will find signing with your child is most useful between 6 and 18 months, before your child has developed a large verbal vocabulary.

YELLOW ● LIGHT

If your child was born prematurely, then at six months old he or she may not yet have the motor development skills needed to begin responding in sign back to you. Though as a parent you might benefit from the extra practice, baby will be ready to begin signing when she begins to hit developmental milestones typical for a six- to eight-month-old child born full-term.

Back

- *Back*, meaning the back of your body, uses the dominant hand.

- Simply tap your back behind the shoulder two times.

- An alternate version of the sign is to finger spell an abbreviated B-C-K. (Refer to the American Manual Alphabet in Chapter 18.) This version is too advanced to use with baby.

- If want to indicate something is moving backwards or to go back, then simply point your dominant thumb behind you and move it backwards two times.

Tummy or Stomach

- Sign *tummy* using your dominant hand.

- Form the letter B with the thumb closed into the palm and the other four fingers extended and pressed together. (Refer to the American Manual Alphabet in Chapter 18.)

- Tap the dominant hand on your tummy two times.

- Alternatively, you can point to your tummy or stomach.

DIAPER TIME
Babies sometimes have their own way of signaling diaper time, but try using ASL

Although it's perfectly fine to go with whatever signs you or your baby develop on your own, don't discount the value of using official American Sign Language signs.

Obviously, there's no magic to ASL as the sign language that babies understand. You could invent your own signs, and used consistently and often, you'd experience the same success. However, teaching your child ASL equips him with the knowledge of the third most widely spoken language in the United States and allows him to be understood by a growing community of ASL users. Not only is ASL the language of the deaf community, it is also used widely in educational and emergency settings.

Diaper

- *Diaper* uses both hands.

- Form the number 3 with both hands using the thumb, index, and middle fingers. (Refer to the number list in Chapter 19.)

- Place both hands at hip level where a diaper would fasten.

- Close together the fingers of the number 3 as though fastening a diaper.

Change

- *Change* uses both hands.

- Each hand forms the letter A with the fist closed and the thumb pointing up. (Refer to the American Manual Alphabet in Chapter 18.)

- Place one fist on top of the other in alternate directions.

- Next, move the fists so they are now alternating in opposite directions.

You will have some exposure to individual ASL signs in this book, but if you would like more information on ASL to communicate with the deaf community, consider checking out an ASL book or taking a class. ASL is an active language that incorporates body language and expression to communicate. ASL does not translate English word for word, but instead tries to convey the overall message of what is being said. ASL does not follow the grammatical rules of English and instead has its own syntax and word order usage.

Clean

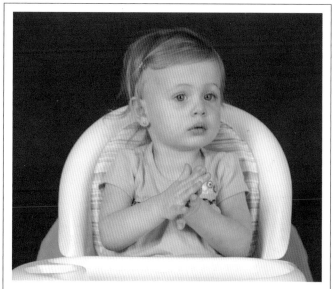

- *Clean* uses both hands.

- Begin with the stationary hand flat, palm facing upwards.

- Slide the dominant hand flat across the stationary hand, with the dominant palm facing the stationary palm.

- Repeat the motion two times as though you are wiping something clean.

Pants

- *Pants* uses both hands.

- Begin with both hands at waist level, palms facing the body.

- Move each hand simultaneously on either leg downwards.

- The hand motion represents each pant leg.

BATH TIME

Bath time is a good start to establishing a comforting and consistent nighttime routine

If your baby is older than four months, then it is important that you have begun to transition your baby's day into a regular routine. Once your child settles into the routine and you have predictable sleep and play times, you will be able to organize your time better as a parent. During those down times you can return calls, do the laundry, and cook meals instead of juggling those tasks during an unorganized day. Babies need a routine so they know what to expect. Routine helps a baby stick to regular feeding times, encouraging baby not to snack, but to have full feedings. When baby is well fed, well loved, and well cared for in a predictable fashion, then you will have created a life of balance for both you and your child.

Bath

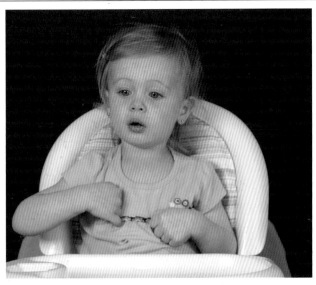

- Form the letter A with both hands. (Refer to the American Manual Alphabet in Chapter 18.)

- Place both hands on the chest.

- Move the hands up and down on the chest as though you are cleaning or scrubbing your chest.

- Use *bath* not only at bath time, but if you are giving a pet a bath or if you are about to take a bath or shower.

Water

- Form the letter W with the dominant hand. (Refer to the American Manual Alphabet in Chapter 18.)

- Bring the W to the bottom of your chin.

- Move it away from and to the chin several times.

- Use *water* for bath time, when your child needs a drink, or even if you are watering your lawn. Take advantage of all opportunities to use this sign.

At nighttime, establish a consistent routine to help cue baby that bedtime is coming. Your nighttime sequence probably involves cuddling, quiet time with baby perhaps while reading a book or rocking in a chair, a soothing bath, and a massage afterwards. Here you will learn the signs *bath*, *water*, *wet*, and *wash*, which you can consistently use as part of the bedtime routine. Before the bath, cue your baby that bath time is coming by talking about and using the signs related to bath time.

No matter what you decide to incorporate into your routine, make sure you stick with it. Last, put baby to sleep at the same time every night. Don't try to wear baby out by keeping him up later. Overstimulating baby can result in a fussy baby who has difficulty settling down.

Wet

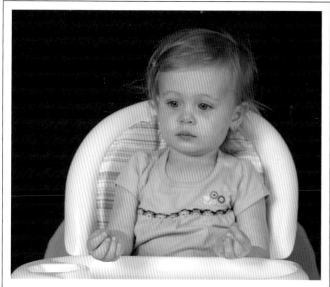

- *Wet* uses both hands.

- Begin with both hands palm up. Close the four fingers to the thumb in an O-like shape.

- Open and close the thumb to the four fingers back and forth while saying, "Wet."

Wash

- *Wash* uses both hands.

- Form both hands into the letter A position. (Refer to the American Manual Alphabet in Chapter 18.)

- Place one hand on top of the other with palms touching. Move the dominant (top) hand in a circular motion on top of the stationary hand. This motion represents washing or scrubbing an item.

- Or, as an alternative, place the dominant hand on the area being washed, like the face or knee, and pretend to scrub the area.

BATHING BLISS

Use the signs *wash face*, *wash hair*, *towel*, and *dry* while bathing baby in the big tub

Bath time is a terrific time to integrate signs into the routine if baby is enjoying the bath. If baby has not yet acclimated to the bath time routine and cries the entire time you are bathing her, it's not time to introduce signs. Don't add more stress to the bathing routine. Your baby should be happy, enjoying the bath time and the attention from mom or dad.

Do you have older children? If big brother or sister wants to join in, welcome the help. Though a parent should always supervise, an older sibling can provide another set of hands to help wash baby. You'll be able to simultaneously teach baby and the older sibling to sign. Best of all, it saves an extra bath later! Here we will learn the signs **wash face, wash hair/**

Wash Face

- Place the dominant hand on the face with the palm facing inward.

- Wipe the hand away from the face as though wiping food or dirt off the face with a napkin.

- Next, move the hand to the other side and repeat the motion.

Wash Hair or Shampoo

- *Wash Hair* or *Shampoo* uses both hands.

- Begin by pretending to pour a bottle of shampoo into one hand.

- Next, place both hands on top of or several inches

away from the top of the head.

- Pretend to wash or scrub the head or hair.

shampoo, towel, and *dry*. As you perform each of these activities, talk with your hands and your voice about what is going on. If baby is cooperative, help baby make the signs as well.

Bath time can be a great winding-down activity before bed, but a cold room can ruin the bath before it begins. Be sure the bathroom is warm. Make sure the water is warm, but not hot to touch on your wrist. Never ever leave baby alone in the tub. If the phone rings, let it ring. If the doorbell rings, let it go. It only takes a second for baby to slip under water and risk drowning. Have an assortment of cups or toys for baby to play with. The kitchen cupboard is a great (and free) resource for bath toys.

Towel

- *Towel* uses both hands.

- Place each hand in a closed fist at about shoulder level.

- Alternately move the hands side to side as though you have a towel behind your back and are drying off with the towel.

- An alternate version of the sign is to draw in the space in front of you a rectangle shape like the shape of a towel.

Dry

- Place your dominant hand in front of your mouth with the index finger extended.

- Your hand will not touch your face, but will be 1 to 2 inches in front of your face. (Don't worry if your child prefers to have her hand touching the face.)

- Next, pull the index finger backwards, bending the finger at both knuckles much like the letter X. (Refer to the American Manual Alphabet in Chapter 18.)

GOING TO SLEEP

Baby still not sleeping? Soothing strategies to help baby sleep through the night

If your baby hasn't yet mastered sleeping through the night, or has recently gotten sick and must re-learn how to sleep through the night, you are probably feeling sleep deprived. Help get back those precious nighttime hours you need to be a better parent and person.

Babies thrive on a consistent routine. Check your day and see if it has become erratic and unpredictable lately. If so, try to restore some order to baby's day. Help baby consistently go to bed at the same time each night. Make sure you are taking advantage of signing as part of this nighttime routine. Whether at bath time, as you read stories, as your child snuggles with his favorite blanket or lovey, or during nighttime

Bed

- *Bed* uses both hands, but your child might find it easier to use just one hand.

- Place the hands together, palms facing each other.

- Next, place the pressed-together palms to the side of the head.

- Gently rest your head against the hands as though you are going to sleep.

Blanket

- *Blanket* uses both hands.

- Begin with both hands folded downward, thumbs tucked inside and palms facing the body.

- For the first part of the sign, both hands are at chest level.

- Simultaneously move both hands upwards to shoulder level.

- The motion will look as though you are pulling up your blanket or covers when in bed.

prayers, use signs both to signal what you are doing and what is coming next. Here you will learn the signs *bed*, *blanket*, *sleep*, and ***prayer,*** which may be core signs for your bedtime routine.

Overstimulation is a common reason why babies can't fall asleep. Check your routine. Perhaps there is too much evening playtime, or a bath may be too stimulating. Begin to wind down and create a calm, peaceful environment.

Throughout the day, give baby time when he is held close to you, either in your arms or in a sling. Babies feel more relaxed next to mom or dad, and this will help keep baby calm as you approach bedtime.

Check out the sleeping environment. When your baby naps, is he sleeping too long? Is the room too dark? While a good three-hour nap may give you sanity during the day, it may be keeping you up at night. Having a well-lit room will encourage a shorter naptime for baby.

Sleep

- *Sleep* uses the dominant hand.

- Place the hand in front of the face (not touching) with fingers spread slightly apart.

- Move the hand downward toward the chin.

- As you move the hand downward, bring all fingers together inward to meet until they touch the thumb.

Prayer

- You may find you already know this popular cultural sign.

- *Prayer* uses both hands.

- Place both hands together, palms pressed together.

- Beyond bedtime, use this sign at church, mealtime, Sunday school, or other appropriate settings.

GRANDPARENTS

Grandparents and extended family can provide extraordinary blessings of support and love for your child

Are grandparents coming for a visit? Here you will learn the signs *grandma*, *grandpa*, *hug*, and *kiss*. Teach your child these signs as you talk about the grandparents' impending visit. During the day when you ask for or give a hug and kiss, use the signs. Grandma and grandpa will be thrilled to use the signs with your child.

If you have grandparents or family who live nearby and want to be involved in your child's life, take advantage of the extra hands and love they can provide. Often these important family members want to help, but don't know how. Be sure to show them the latest signs you are working with so they, too, can participate in baby's growing communication skills.

Grandma

- *Grandma* uses the dominant hand.

- Place the hand in a number 5 position with all fingers outstretched. Touch the thumb to the bottom of the chin.

- Wiggle the fingers.

- The signs *mom*, *grandma*, and *girl* are all based on the bottom of the face.

Grandpa

- *Grandpa* uses the dominant hand.

- Place the hand in a number 5 position with all fingers outstretched. Touch the thumb to the forehead.

- Wiggle the fingers back and forth.

- Notice that *dad*, *grandpa*, and *boy* are all signed in the forehead region.

It's always a good idea to let the family members know your house rules, but be careful of how you communicate them. Always remember that what your loved one is doing or saying is motivated by love. Though you may not want to hear unsolicited advice, be courteous, knowing they are just trying to help. The more people to love your child just means the more your child is loved.

BABY'S WORLD

Hug

- Hug uses both arms and hands.

- Cross both arms and hands in front of the chest making an X shape.

- Squeeze the arms into the body as though you are hugging someone.

- This sign is very close to the sign for *love*, which makes the same motion without the hugging action.

- Make the hugging motion two times.

Kiss

- Begin by making a kissing motion and sound with your lips.

- While making that motion, close both hands so that the fingertips and thumbs are touching.

- Next bring both hands together so the fingertips touch, then pull the hands apart again much like a kiss between two people.

SIBLINGS
Siblings can provide great modeling for your child's development

Does your baby have an older brother or sister? Siblings provide so many great opportunities for learning. Your baby will be captivated by his big brother and sister and will want to be like them. Siblings can help encourage littler ones to try to do and say more. Here you will learn the signs *sister* and

brother. Encourage the older kids to use the signs when they are talking about each other.

By nine months your child's motor development is rapidly improving. Take some time to check your child's development according to typical milestones for this age.

Sister: Part One

- *Sister* uses both hands.

- Begin with the dominant hand on the chin. Place the hand on the same side of the chin as the hand you are using.

- The hand can either be in the letter L shape or in a fist with the thumb extended. (Refer to the American Manual Alphabet in Chapter 18.)

Sister: Part Two

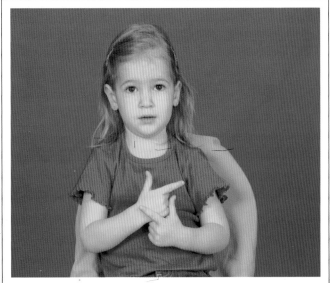

- Next, diagonally move the dominant hand downward until it rests on the stationary hand, which is at chest level.

- Both hands will end in the letter L position, with the index finger and thumb extended.

- Signs that indicate female gender, such as *mom*, *grandmother*, *girl*, or *sister*, are all focused around the chin area.

26

9-month milestone check

Physical:

Begins to rock on all fours, scoot, or perhaps even crawl.

May be able to pull up to a standing position.

Most babies will be able to sit up without support.

May grasp objects with thumb and first or second finger.

Be able to move objects back and forth from hand to hand.

Cognitive:

Baby is beginning to talk to you through the use of sounds, emotions, hands, and hopefully signs.

Baby may develop a fear of strangers. If you leave baby with a sitter or grandparent, baby may cry initially.

You should talk to your doctor if your baby:

Does not attempt to roll over, or shows no interest in rolling over or sitting.

Does not reach for objects or puts objects in mouth.

Does not make babbling sounds or imitate sounds.

Cannot bear weight on his legs when held in a standing position.

Does not respond to visual stimulation or sounds.

Brother: Part One

- Like the sign for *sister, brother* uses both hands and makes a similar sign.

- For *brother*, begin with the dominant hand on the forehead. The hand can either be in a closed fist with the thumb extended or in the letter L shape.

- The dominant hand should be on the same side of the forehead as the hand you are signing with.

- Hold the stationary hand at chest level.

Brother: Part Two

- Next, diagonally move the dominant hand downward until it rests on the stationary hand, which is at chest level.

- Both hands will end in the letter L position, with the index finger and thumb extended.

- Signs that indicate male gender, such as *father, grandfather, boy,* and *brother*, are all focused around the forehead area.

RESPONSES & COMMANDS
Playing and signing with baby is a great opportunity to bond while developing motor skills

The words *yes, no, look* and **stay** are words your child is probably becoming very familiar with. Here you will learn the signs for these high usage responses and commands.

Getting down on the floor and playing while signing with baby not only helps connect you and your child, but helps your child's motor skill development. Your baby may already be crawling, or very close to it. Crawling, scooting, and squirming begin with first being able to get up on the hands and knees. Once he has mastered that trick, he'll figure out how to rock back and forth on his knees. After some practice baby begins to figure out how to crawl. Try encouraging baby to chase you by crawling to and away from your baby, enticing

Yes

- While *yes* can certainly be signed with a head nod up and down, there is a way to say *yes* using one hand.

- Form the letter S. (Refer to the American Manual Alphabet in Chapter 18.)

- From the wrist, move the hand up and down several times. Make sure the tone of your voice is paired with the sign.

No

- Like *yes*, *no* can be signed by shaking your head side to side, but can also be signed using one hand.

- Extend the index finger, middle finger, and thumb. Keep the remaining two fingers closed.

- Touch the thumb to the index and middle finger several times. This opening and closing motion is the ASL sign for *no*.

him to follow you. Even if your baby isn't crawling yet, he'll want to chase after you and will be motivated to try.

To encourage hand-eye coordination, lay several toys out in front of baby for her to explore and discover. Include a range of textures and sounds. If baby is beginning to experiment with crawling, place some of the items just beyond reach to encourage her to reach out and grab them.

Play peek-a-boo by covering yourself completely with a blanket and having baby pull the blanket off. Your baby will learn cause and effect while delighting in this new game.

Look

- Form the letter V with the dominant hand. (Refer to the American Manual Alphabet in Chapter 18.)

- Begin by placing the letter V just outside the eyes.

- Bring the V away from the face several inches. Swivel the V outward to face away from the body. The motion should look as though the fingers are now watching something else.

Stay

- *Stay* uses one or both hands.

- Form the letter Y. (Refer to the American Manual Alphabet in Chapter 18.)

- Place the Y at about chest level.

- Move the Y back towards and away from your body several times. Make sure that your tone reflects the command to stay.

BABY'S WORLD

IMITATION PLAY

What kind of parent are you? Be a parent worthy of emulating

It is fun to watch your child pick up a ball and throw it back, imitating your play. You can almost see the lightbulb going on as baby tries to mimic your actions, words, and signs.

One of the scariest moments of being a parent is the realization of how much you are being watched. What you eat, how much you exercise, what you say, how you act, and how you give will not only be observed for a lifetime but will also be imitated. The actions you take don't just affect you; they help determine the person your child will ultimately become. This can inspire us to be better role models, from how we eat, to how we respond to the needy, to how we talk to our spouses.

Give: Part One

- *Give* uses one or both hands.

- Begin with hands folded with thumbs touching fingers.

- Hands will begin their motion at chest level.

Give: Part Two

- Move hands outward simultaneously.

- If you wanted to say *give* to everyone, then make the motion outward to one side, to the center, and to the next side.

- To indicate someone gave you something, reverse the motion. Begin with the hands extended outward and move the hands toward your body.

Modeling after Mom and Dad starts early. During playtime, mimicking Mom and Dad is a normal part of growing and developing. Around 12 months of age, your child will probably be able to pick up a play telephone and pretend to talk on the phone or cradle a baby doll. Some of the earliest actions your child will imitate are *give*, *take*, and *ball*, which are the signs taught here.

Taken inventory of your life lately? What areas in your life do you want to improve or change? Holding onto any bad habits like smoking or overeating? While your child is still young, take the opportunity to try to become the person you want to be, and more importantly, to cultivate the traits you want your child to one day emulate.

Take

- *Take* uses the dominant hand.

- Begin with the hand and arm extended away from your body. Slightly bend your hand.

- Move the hand toward your body. As you move the hand, draw your fingers together in a fist-like shape as though you are grabbing something.

Ball

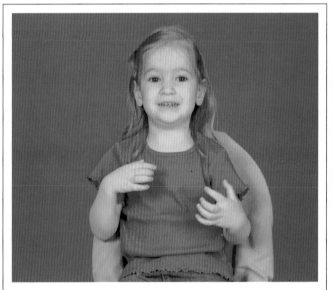

- *Ball* uses both hands.

- Form each hand with the palms facing each other, fingers spaced apart.

- Your hands should appear to be holding an imaginary ball.

- Move the hands slightly back and forth representing a ball-like shape.

FIRST FEELINGS
Equip your child to express how she is feeling

Without words or signs, babies must communicate through tears—tears over being hungry, tired, thirsty, bored, over-stimulated, and more. Often, despite every effort, parents still can't figure out what exactly is wrong and why baby is crying. Through sign, your baby will have a means to communicate to you, minimizing those teary moments.

Through sign language you are giving your child a non-verbal way to communicate her ideas, desires, and needs. Increasing communication can help baby feel more content and adjusted.

Here you will learn the signs *happy*, *nice*, *hurt*, and *mad*. These signs will help baby communicate to you how she is

Happy

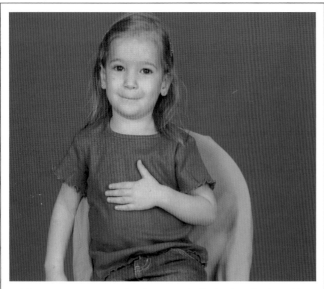

- *Happy* can use one or both hands.

- Place hands on chest, palm facing towards the chest.

- Circle the hand or hands simultaneously and in the same direction.

Nice

- *Nice* is similar to the sign for *clean*.

- The stationary hand faces upward with a flat palm. This hand does not move.

- Hold the dominant hand flat and sweep it across the stationary hand.

feeling. One of the hallmarks of ASL in the deaf community is the use of facial expressions in conjunction with the signs. Go ahead and integrate that same principle here. Being expressive with your face and tone will help communicate to baby what these words mean. When you sign the word *happy*, be sure you are smiling and visibly look happy. If you sign *hurt*, make a sad, in-pain face. You get the picture. Your emotion and voice are as important as the actual sign to convey meaning. You might feel silly at first acting so animated, but consider the end result and get into the role!

Hurt

- *Hurt* uses both hands.

- Extend each index finger out. Point the fingers opposite one another.

- Next, simultaneously but in alternating directions twist the wrists.

- To help convey the meaning of the sign, demonstrate a pained expression as you sign the word.

Mad

- *Mad* uses the dominant hand.

- Place the hand several inches away from the face. The fingers are spread apart and the hand is slightly bent.

- Move the tips of the fingers back and forth.

- Make sure the expression on your face matches the expression in your tone as well as the sign.

CAR RIDE

Car trips are an exciting part of baby's day; use signs to get him prepared

Though you shouldn't sign while driving, you can use signs to prepare baby for an outing and get him excited about it. The signs used here—*car*, *seat*, *buckle*, and *safe*—are all great signs to use when talking about going for a car ride and getting into the car. These signs can be used every day at every outing and in anticipation of an outing.

While you're teaching your child about car safety, take some time to review your own adherence to safety guidelines. What kind of car seat are you using now? An infant, rear-facing car seat can be used until your baby is around 20 to 22 pounds. After your baby has outgrown the infant car seat, look into convertible car seats. Keep your baby rear-facing as long as

Car

- *Car* uses both hands.

- Pretend to grip the steering wheel of a car. Grip both hands around the imaginary wheel.

- Move the hands side to side as though you are steering the imaginary steering wheel.

Car Seat

- *Car seat* uses both hands, and is a combination sign.

- First, begin by making the sign for *car* (see previous picture).

- Next, make the sign for *seat*, which is made by using both hands in the letter H position with the index and

middle finger extended. (Refer to the American Manual Alphabet in Chapter 18.)

- The hands begin about shoulder width apart. Move the dominant extended fingers to rest or sit on top of the stationary extended fingers. Palms face down.

possible. The American Academy of Pediatrics recommends children continue to ride rear-facing until they are at least one year of age and a minimum of 20 pounds. After your baby is over 30 pounds, or when his head is about an inch away from the top of the seat, it is time to turn the car seat front-facing. The placement of the car seat clip or buckle is important. For maximum protection for baby, place the clip around armpit level, not too high on the neck and not too low over the belly.

••••••••••••••••• RED ● LIGHT •••••••••••••••••
Never place a rear-facing car seat in the front seat where an active airbag could deploy. When choosing a car seat, avoid hand-me-downs and bargain-basement deals. Do your research and keep your receipt. The harness should fit tightly on your child, and the seat should be secure in the car. Visit www.nhtsa.dot.gov/cps/cpsfitting/index .cfm to find a Child Safety Seat Inspection Station to be sure your car seat is fitting properly.

Buckle

- *Buckle* uses both hands in the letter H position. The middle finger and index finger are extended.

- Begin with both hands at waist level, slightly apart.

- Next, move the hands together so that the dominant fingers are resting in front of the stationary fingers. This will resemble a belt or seatbelt being buckled.

Safe

- *Safe* uses both hands and arms.

- Begin with both arms crossed, much like the *love* sign. Each hand's fingers are open and spread apart, with the palms flat and facing the body.

- Move both hands and arms apart until the arms are no longer crossed, but straight directly in front of the chest.

- The hands transition from the open hand to a closed fist.

WINDING DOWN
Lulling conversations while using soothing signs help set the mood for saying goodnight

The nighttime routine is a source of comfort for baby. Whether you bathe first, read stories first, share a bedtime prayer, or spend a little time cuddling together, those cues let baby know that the busy day has come to an end.

Here we will learn *read*, *pick*, *book*, and *again*. Don't worry about learning signs that don't apply to your lifestyle or routine. Since signing success with a baby depends on consistency, it's important to use the signs that best integrate into your normal routine and to use them often. The goal is for baby to be able to communicate with you with meaningful signs for her world.

As you talk, soothe, or sing to baby at night, she might try

Read

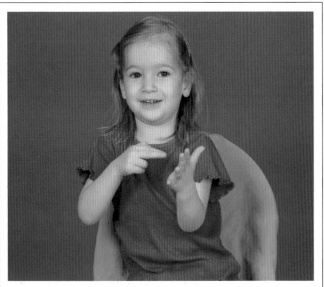

- *Read* uses both hands.

- Form the letter V with the dominant hand using the index and middle fingers extended and apart in the V shape. The remaining fingers will be folded down. (Refer to the American Manual Alphabet in Chapter 18.)

- The stationary hand will be flat, palm facing upwards, representing a page being read.

- Place the V at the top of the stationary hand, about an inch away. Move the hand downward towards the wrist, representing that a page has been read.

Pick or Choose

- *Pick* uses the dominant hand.

- Begin with the palm facing away from your body at about chest level with all fingers loosely spread apart.

- Close the fingers as though you were picking something up between the thumb and index finger.

- This sign is helpful when selecting a book, a toy, a snack, and more.

to talk back to you. Many of her sounds may mimic yours and often her facial expressions will mirror yours as well. Though your baby may not understand everything you are saying, she will understand a soothing tone, an angry tone, or an excited tone. Be sure your tone is communicating your message. Your baby is probably beginning to babble repetitive sounds such as *ba-ba-ba* or *da-da* or *ma-ma*. Encourage baby's words by repeating these sounds back to her and leading her to try new ones. Keep the back and forth rapport going to encourage verbal communication.

Book

- *Book* uses both hands.

- Begin with both hands touching, palms facing one another.

- Fold open the hands as though they are a book being opened. The hands touch at the pinky fingers, and palms are flat, facing upwards.

Again

- *Again* uses both hands.

- Hold the stationary hand flat and straight, all fingers pressed together.

- The dominant hand is bent. Strike the fingertips against the stationary palm.

- *Again* is helpful to use at story time, when singing a song, playing a game, or more.

BUSY BABY

FARM ANIMALS

Whether in a book, as puppets, as toys, or real, barnyard animals are just plain fun

Animals pique baby's curiosity. Babies love to hear, look at, and touch animals. Whether you are headed for a day at the petting zoo or a farm, or just going for an adventure in a book, learning signs for these animals will help broaden baby's signing vocabulary. Here we will learn *farm*, *cow*, *horse*, and *pig*.

As your child begins to play with toy animals or other manipulatives, or to pick up finger foods, you may have begun to notice handedness. By 12 to 18 months old, baby will begin to hold an object with one hand and touch and play with the object with the other hand. After 18 months old, hand preference begins to become a bit more defined and noticeable.

Farm

- *Farm* uses the dominant hand.

- Form the number 4 by bending the thumb across the palm with the remaining fingers extended. (Refer to the number list in Chapter 19.)

- Move the hand across the chin.

Cow

- *Cow* uses one or both hands.

- Form the letter Y: Extend the pinky and thumb, and close the middle three fingers. (Refer to the American Manual Alphabet in Chapter 18.)

- Place the thumb of the Y on the temple of the forehead. If you are using your right hand, you'll place it on the right temple. If you are left-handed you'll use the left temple.

- Rotate the hand forward and back, pivoting on the thumb.

Whether your child is left- or right-handed will not influence his ability to sign. Allow your baby to sign with the hand he feels most comfortable using. Don't try to force your child to switch hand preference; instead, allow him to discover the best fit for him.

Help your child develop his fine motor skills by giving him a variety of objects to grasp. During playtime, give your baby different textures and small toys with which to interact. As your child gets a little bigger, age-appropriate toys with dials, switches, and levers can help fine motor development.

Horse

- *Horse* uses one or both hands.

- Fold the ring and pinky finger down. Extend the thumb, and keep the index and middle finger straight with no space between them.

- Next, place the thumb on the temple. Like *cow*, use the same side of the face as the hand in use.

- Move the index finger and middle finger back and forth simultaneously.

Pig

- *Pig* uses the dominant hand.

- Face the palm toward the ground.

- Simply place the hand underneath the chin. Fold the fingers downward and then extend the fingers straight again. Repeat.

- To have fun with this sign, consider adding pig noises as you make the sign and say "Pig."

ZOO ANIMALS

Zoo animals are large, make fun sounds, and are interesting to sign

A great way to introduce zoo animals without ever leaving home is to visit the animals in a book! Reading aloud with your baby is a fun, shared activity. You'll enjoy the quiet cuddly moments, while baby has the opportunity to learn about new concepts and understand the meaning of words. This activity will also model reading to your child. The more exposure your child has to words and sounds, the more equipped she will be to acquire verbal skills. Here you will learn the signs for *zoo*, *lion*, *monkey*, and *giraffe*. Show animation with your voice and face as you sign these words, helping convey more about these animals—what they look and sound like.

Use what you already know. While you read, pick words in each book that you can sign. Help baby sign the words as well. Repeat reading the book often. Your baby will learn how

Zoo

- *Zoo* uses the dominant hand to form the letters Z-O-O in quick succession. (Refer to the American Manual Alphabet in Chapter 18.)

- Z is formed by using the index finger to draw the letter Z in the space in front of you.

- O is formed by closing all fingers to touch the thumb, making a round O shape.

- Your child may end up reinventing this sign by wiggling the index finger. Adapting the signs for your child is perfectly fine.

Lion

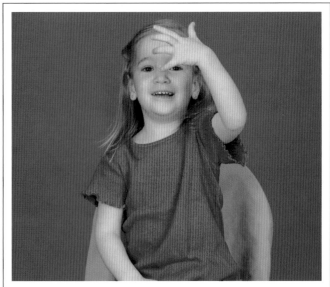

- *Lion* uses the dominant hand.

- The motion you will make will represent the mane of a male lion.

- Use the whole hand with fingers slightly cupped and bent palm facing the head.

- Starting at the forehead move your hand to the back of your head, mimicking the shape of a lion's mane.

to predict what comes next in the book and will quickly learn the sign you are teaching. Reading is a wonderful teachable opportunity to integrate sign language.

Don't get discouraged if baby isn't always interested in reading. Sometimes the edges of a book seem more entertaining than the actual pictures. For a baby less than 12 months old, focus on simple pictures and simple stories. Save the elaborate stories for when your child is a little older. Soon baby will be pointing, signing at objects, and trying to turn the pages for you.

To encourage reading, make sure books are accessible around the house. As your child gets older, having books readily available encourages baby to pick one out and prompt a reading moment with you.

Monkey

- *Monkey* uses both hands.

- Place both hands on either side of the waist. Keep the hands cupped with fingers slightly apart.

- From the wrist, move the hands slightly up and down.

- Have fun with this sign by making monkey noises. The more fun you have with the sign, the more fun it will be for baby to imitate.

Giraffe

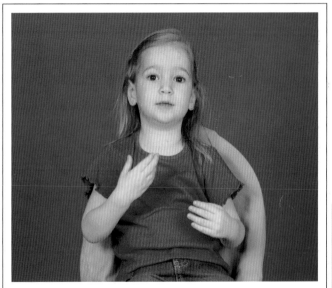

- *Giraffe* uses the dominant hand.

- Form the letter C. (Refer to the American Manual Alphabet in Chapter 18.)

- Place the C at the bottom of your neck or mid-chest area, about an inch or two away from your body.

- Move the hand upward, indicating the very long neck of a giraffe.

- Talk about the giraffe's long neck as you make the sign so the child makes the connection.

CREEPY CRAWLIES

Outdoor insects are interesting. Help keep baby safe while playing outside

Heading outdoors? Going outside provides many great signing opportunities. Look up for planes or helicopters; look down and see bugs, grass, plants, and flowers. Go to the park and see swings, slides, and obstacles to climb. Your child will be excited to be outside and will be in an environment conducive to signing. Here you will learn the signs for *spider*, *bug*,

snake, and ***butterfly.*** Not only can you use these signs outside at the zoo, park, or even in your own backyard, but also look for books featuring stories about outdoor critters. Use your signs every time you see or talk about these creatures and be creative with your voice and facial expression.

Before you head outside, it's always a good idea to make

Spider

As your hands move forward simultaneously, they should resemble a spider scurrying away.

Bug

- *Spider* is a fun sign using both hands.

- Begin with both hands crossed at the wrists.

- Wiggle the fingers as both hands move forward, much like a spider would skitter across the floor.

- Use expression in your voice as you describe these creepy crawly creatures.

- *Bug* uses the dominant hand.

- Form the ASL number 3 using the thumb, index finger and middle finger. (Refer to the number list in Chapter 19.)

- Place the thumb on the side of the nose. Use the right side of the nose if you are using your right hand, left side if using left hand.

- Wiggle the index and middle fingers back and forth.

sure baby is ready to face the elements. Hats and long sleeves help fend off the sun's rays. Sunscreen is a must for sensitive baby skin. Look for physical or chemical-free sunscreens, which tend not to irritate baby's skin as much as chemical sunscreens. The American Association of Pediatrics recommends a minimum of 15 sun protection factor (SPF). Be mindful how long you are outside. If baby is starting to walk, make sure those little feet are protected.

YELLOW LIGHT

Most of the time, bug bites or stings are harmless. Aside from the discomfort from the bite or sting, your baby should be okay. Occasionally some children will show an allergic reaction to a bite or sting. If your child reacts with vomiting, difficulty breathing or labored breathing, swelling of lips and throat, or a rash or hives, then immediate medical care is required. Call 911 for immediate response.

Snake

- *Snake* uses the dominant hand.

- Make a bent letter V. (Refer to the American Manual Alphabet in Chapter 18.) The bend in the fingers represents the fangs of the snake.

- Begin with the hand at waist level. Move the arm and hand outward in a curving motion, much like a snake would slither.

Butterfly

- *Butterfly* uses both hands.

- Interlock both thumbs, crossing the wrists and connecting one hand to the other.

- Move the fingers back and forth simultaneously, representing the wings of the butterfly.

- Move the hands around, much like a butterfly would fly.

BUSY BABY

JOY OF MUSIC
Learn signs, explore sounds, and have fun through music

Now that your baby is getting a little older, introducing music into your playtime is a great activity. Rattles that shake and make noise, or a baby drum set with sticks to tap with, teach baby a cause-and-effect relationship. Your child is now also able to effectively hold and grasp objects, helping to hone fine motor development. In the car take advantage of some great sing-along songs. Exposing your baby to a variety of

musical instruments for experimentation, as well as a buffet of musical styles from classical to country, helps your baby's brain develop neural synapses.

While you and your child are enjoying music, use that time to explore signs, too. Here you will learn the signs *music*, *drum*, *guitar*, and *sing*. As you play music, make the *music* sign and talk about how you are listening to music. Or if your

Music

- *Music* uses the dominant hand and the stationary arm.

- Place the stationary arm directly in front of you.

- Using the dominant hand, sweep the hand back and forth down the length of the stationary arm.

- Make the motion several times.

Drum

- *Drum* uses both hands.

- Both hands will appear to be holding imaginary drumsticks.

- Make the motion of beating the drum with both hands.

- Because this sign is so similar to the motion your child makes when playing the drums, it will make sense and be an easy sign to learn.

child is beating away in delight on a play keyboard or drums, use your hands and voice to tell your child what wonderful music he is making. As with all signs, be consistent with your approach. These are easy signs to learn, and will not only help baby explore body movement more, but will also give baby a means to communicate when he wants to have fun with music and sounds.

Guitar

- "Guitar" uses both hands and arms.

- Much like "drums," "guitar" emulates the motion of playing a guitar.

- The stationary arm and hand hold the imaginary guitar.

- The dominant hand strums the strings on the imaginary guitar.

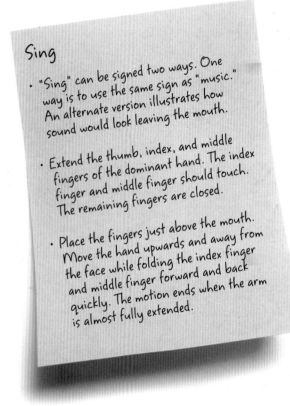

Sing

- "Sing" can be signed two ways. One way is to use the same sign as "music." An alternate version illustrates how sound would look leaving the mouth.

- Extend the thumb, index, and middle fingers of the dominant hand. The index finger and middle finger should touch. The remaining fingers are closed.

- Place the fingers just above the mouth. Move the hand upwards and away from the face while folding the index finger and middle finger forward and back quickly. The motion ends when the arm is almost fully extended.

BUSY BABY

THE HEAVENS ABOVE

Not turning or responding to those outdoor noises?
Know the signs of infant hearing loss

Taking your baby for a walk outside and letting her crawl on the grass or swing in the park is good for both of you. Take time to point out what you see and to teach new signs, such as *star*, *sun*, *moon*, and *rainbow*. There are also many interesting sounds, such as chirping crickets, croaking toads, and singing birds. But what happens when baby doesn't respond to the sounds? Hearing loss may develop post-birth due to wax buildup or chronic ear infections. While sometimes the hearing loss may be temporary, severe ear infections can cause permanent hearing loss. Recognizing the signs of hearing loss is imperative for early diagnosis and treatment. Schedule a hearing screening if you see the following red flags:

Star

- *Star* uses both hands.

- Form the number 1 with both index fingers extended. (Refer to the number list in Chapter 19.)

- Face the palms outward, away from your body.

- Alternately brush one hand against the other.

- Use this sign when you are outside at night and when you are reading about stars.

Sun

- *Sun* uses the dominant hand.

- Begin by forming the letter C. (Refer to the American Manual Alphabet in Chapter 18.)

- Place the C several inches away from your temple. Use the same side of your body as the hand you are using.

- Move the hand outward, toward the sky, to represent the sun in the sky.

Does not wake up to loud noises such as a door slam, an alarm going off, a train whistle, or other loud noises.
Does not startle or cry to surprising loud noises.
Does not turn toward you when you speak.
Does not try to mimic sounds you make.
Does not babble or coo.

Early diagnosis and treatment can help maximize any residual hearing your child may have with the use of hearing aids or other devices. Further, the earlier you are aware of hearing loss the sooner you can educate yourself and begin to adapt your parenting methods for your child. While deafness may not have been what you imagined or envisioned for your child, it can simply be a different outcome. The deaf community is full of educated, resourceful individuals who see their lives as being full of ability, not disability.

Moon

Many signs, like moon, are iconic, meaning they mimic the real life object.

- *Moon* uses the dominant hand.

- Cup the thumb and index finger while keeping the remaining fingers closed.

- Begin with motion at about eye level and form an arc forward, much like the shape of a crescent moon.

- Repeat the sign as you say the word several times to reinforce the word.

Rainbow

- "Rainbow" uses the dominant hand.

- Form the number 4 with your thumb in your palm and the rest of the fingers extended. (Refer to the number list in Chapter 19.) Use the hand to make a rainbow-like shape at about chest level.

- Wiggle the fingers slightly as you make the arc from one side to the other.

- Your child may end up using one finger or the whole hand to say this sign. Perfection isn't necessary; just making an effort is success!

EVERYDAY PLAY

How's your baby playing and growing? Developmental milestones for a 12-month-old

Playtime is an essential part of baby's growth and development. Here we will cover great signs for imitation play: *puppet*, *doll*, *telephone*, and *camera*. By 12 months your child should have interest in some of these items or be able to imitate sounds back to you. As a parent, observation during playtime is important. If baby hasn't quite mastered some milestones, perhaps your child needs to have more floor time. If baby isn't responding with sounds, then spend a little more time with your child one on one encouraging verbal exploration. It's always a good idea to look at developmental milestones to be sure your baby is on track.

Before you head to the doctor for your child's 12-month

Puppet

- *Puppet* is an easy sign using the dominant hand.

- Form a C shape with the dominant hand. Next, open and close the hand touching the thumb to the rest of the fingers much like a person might naturally gesture to describe someone talking.

- This motion represents the motion a hand makes while using a puppet.

Doll

- *Doll* uses the dominant hand.

- Form the letter X by bending the index finger. All other fingers will remain closed. (Refer to the American Manual Alphabet in Chapter 18.)

- Place the finger on the top of the nose and move it downward two times.

- Use this sign for baby dolls, Barbie dolls, rag dolls, or action figures.

visit, take a moment to review typical milestones and see if there are any areas of concern.

12-month milestone check

Physical:

Birth weight has tripled.

Baby is able to pull up to stand.

Baby begins to walk with or without assistance.

Baby can grasp items between thumb and index finger (pincer grasp).

Cognitive:

Baby responds to his name when called.

Baby can say "Mama" or "Dada," in addition to two other words.

Baby is able to wave bye-bye.

Baby can understand and obey simple commands.

Baby can point to objects.

Baby can understand some words.

Telephone

- This simple sign is probably one you already know.

- Using your dominant hand form the letter Y with the thumb and pinky extended and the rest of the fingers closed. (Refer to the American Manual Alphabet in Chapter 18.)

- Place the hand next to the head with the pinky near the mouth and the thumb near the ear, as though talking on a phone.

Camera

- *Camera* uses both hands.

- Both hands frame the index finger and thumb around the eye region of the face.

- The dominant index finger pretends to push a button as though it is snapping a picture.

- Use this sign when you want to take a picture or when your child is playing with his own toy camera.

PETS
Help baby learn about how to treat the animals in your home

Do you have a pet in your home? Most babies can't get enough of the dog or cat. Unfortunately, baby's curiosity may mean the cat ends up being patted too hard, or the dog's tail gets pulled. Learning how to safely interact with house pets is an important part of growing up with animals. Here we will learn the signs *dog* and *cat*.

Now that baby is becoming more mobile it is important to take a few safety precautions. Make sure your pet's feeding area is out of baby's reach. Not only can the food be a possible choking hazard for baby, but the animal will see the baby's presence as a threat and invasion of his territory. Other areas where baby should never be are dog crates or kennels, cat litter boxes, and pet beds. Prevent unwanted provocations by using a baby gate, or by feeding the animal in a room

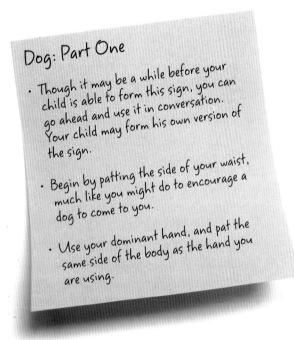

Dog: Part One

- Though it may be a while before your child is able to form this sign, you can go ahead and use it in conversation. Your child may form his own version of the sign.

- Begin by patting the side of your waist, much like you might do to encourage a dog to come to you.

- Use your dominant hand, and pat the same side of the body as the hand you are using.

Dog: Part Two

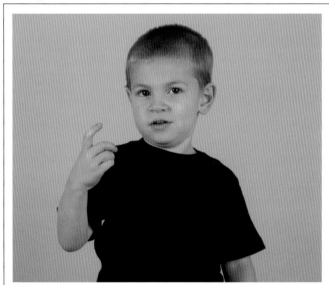

- After making the patting motion, you will then snap.

- Form the snap with the same hand with which you made the first patting motion.

- Your child may just use the patting motion to sign *dog*, which is perfectly fine.

- Be sure to make dog sounds while you make this sign to make it more fun!

(like laundry room or garage) that is off-limits for baby. Never leave the animal alone in the room with baby. Either one may decide to become a little too curious and physical. Observe how your animal is interacting with the baby. If you see signs of defensive behavior, consider dog training or talk to your veterinarian. Keeping baby safe is always your first priority.

If you don't already have a pet, now probably isn't the best time to introduce one into the home. A new baby is a wonderful addition to the family, but it also brings added stress, demands, change, and disruption. Compounding this with the addition of a new pet will only intensify those feelings. Additionally, your child will better appreciate the interaction and responsibility of a pet when she is several years older.

Cat: Part One

- *Cat* uses the dominant hand.

- Use the index finger and thumb. All other fingers remain closed.

- Pretend the index finger and thumb are closed on a whisker of the cat on the side of the mouth.

Cat: Part Two

- Imagine that each finger is pinched on either side of a whisker.

- Pull the fingers away from the side of the face as though they were feeling the length of the cat whisker.

- As you make the sign, ask questions like, "What does the cat say?" followed by a "Meow."

STORYBOOK CREATURES
Using puppets to bring storybook creatures to life is fun and stimulates verbal development

Storybooks create a wonderful window of opportunity for a child. No matter where a person lives, she can escape to a faraway land, an enchanted forest, or a barn full of animals. Here we will learn four common storybook animals: *mouse*, *turtle*, *rooster*, and *frog*.

After you've read a favorite story to your child, why not take the characters to the next level through puppet play? In your toy collection you might consider purchasing several puppets to use for stories, playtime, and even mealtime.

Puppets don't have to be purchased. Puppets can be made easily and inexpensively right at home with socks, paper bags, or even a sticker on the tip of your finger (but be careful

Mouse

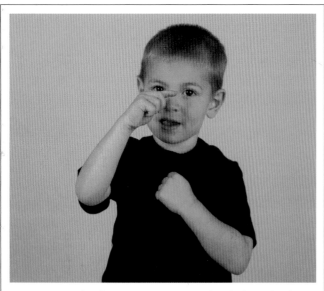

- *Mouse* uses the dominant hand.

- Form the number 1 with the index finger extended. All other fingers will remain closed. (Refer to the number list in Chapter 19.)

- Next, brush the index finger back and forth over the tip of the nose.

Turtle

- *Turtle* uses both hands.

- The dominant hand forms a closed fist with the thumb facing upward.

- Cover the dominant hand with the stationary hand. This represents the shell of the turtle.

- The thumb should be peeking out underneath the stationary hand. Wiggle the thumb back and forth to represent the turtle's head.

about using small buttons or other potential choking hazards). Creating a puppet can be as simple or as extravagant as you want it to be.

Begin with a simple story and use puppets to either act as characters in the story, or to narrate the story. In addition to stimulating verbal development through interactive story telling, puppets are also a source of tactile stimulation, providing a variety of textures, from fur to paper to cotton and more, for your child to explore. Puppets can also be helpful when feeding a fussy baby or be a fun activity for a rainy day.

Hide puppets around the house and have your child play hide and seek!

Puppets are great for story time and so much more. If you have new family or friends coming over, consider using puppets to help break the ice. Children who may not respond to an adult immediately tend to be less shy and more responsive when puppets are used. Additionally, puppets are a great tool to reinforce rules by having the puppet state the rule or talk about an issue that is important to you.

Rooster

- *Rooster* uses the dominant hand.

- Form the ASL number 3 with the thumb, index finger, and middle finger extended. The remaining fingers are folded closed. (Refer to the number list in Chapter 19.)

- Place the thumb on the center of the forehead.

- Rotate the hand back and forth from the wrist to represent the rooster's comb.

Frog

- *Frog* uses the dominant hand.

- Form the number 2 with the dominant hand.

- Place the 2 underneath your chin.

- Fold the extended fingers of the 2 back and forth and again two times.

- Have fun with this sign, making frog noises in conjunction with the sign.

GOING OUT
Taking a vacation? Learn signs for getting dressed and tips for extended travel

Waking up and getting dressed are part of your child's normal routine. Daily routine signs can be repeated consistently and have the potential to be the signs that baby will use the most. Here we will learn *brush hair*, *coat*, *shirt*, and *dress*.

What about when you have to think about more than getting dressed for today, for instance packing and traveling for vacation? While vacations may not be as carefree as they were before baby, traveling with your child can still be a fun getaway.

The difference between a great vacation and a very bad idea is how prepared you are. First, plan for a family friendly location. You'll want to go somewhere you feel welcomed

Brush Hair

- The sign for *brush hair* uses the dominant hand.

- Simply hold a pretend brush in the dominant hand and act as though you are brushing your hair from the top of the head to the bottom.

- Use the same side of the head as the hand you are using.

- Use this sign as you are getting ready and as you help baby get ready for the day.

Coat

- *Coat* uses both hands.

- Begin with both hands in a closed fist with the thumbs extending upwards.

- Place both hands at the shoulders.

- Move the hands simultaneously toward each other as though you are putting on a coat.

and wanted. Whether flying or driving, packing a survival bag is paramount to success. Include ample diapers, wipes, more snacks than baby could possibly eat, plenty of bottles or juice, baby's security object, backup pacifiers, new toys to spark interest, and familiar toys to calm baby down. Pack needed medications and have a list of medical providers for your destination should baby get sick. If you are driving, schedule breaks often when baby is awake and drive the distance during sleeping time.

When you arrive at your destination, be sure that you stick to baby's routine as much as possible. Altering naptime and bedtime can make baby fussy, cause nighttime wakefulness, and ruin a perfectly good vacation. During baby's naptimes alternate who gets to hit the pool, or research together what next adventure to try. Or, better yet, nap with baby and relax on your vacation! Last, have realistic expectations of what your vacation will look like so you don't set yourself up for disappointment later.

The sign for "dress" can be used for both the noun and verb.

Shirt

- *Shirt* uses both hands.

- Place your hands just below the shoulders.

- Using the index fingers and thumbs of each hand, slightly tug at your shirt.

Dress

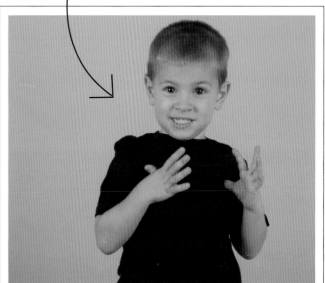

- *Dress* uses both hands.

- Begin the motion with both hands at about shoulder level. Hands are open with all fingers extended. Palms face the body.

- Move both hands simul-taneously downwards the length of the chest.

- In ASL the context of the conversation helps clarify if this sign is being used to describe the act of getting dressed or the piece of clothing that is worn.

SHOES & SOCKS
Protect those tiny toes with shoes and socks

Heading outside? As you protect that precious head and tiny feet from the outdoor elements, use these easy signs for *shoes*, *socks*, and *hat*.

Around the time baby begins to pull up the inevitable question arises. "Does my child need shoes?" When a baby is learning to walk and the child is in a safe indoor setting, there is absolutely no reason for shoes. Buying shoes because you think your child will benefit from the support of the shoe is incorrect.

Your baby's foot is the best tool she can have when she is learning to walk. The foot is designed to carry the weight of a person and is built to grip surfaces like the floor. When you

Shoes: Part One

- The sign for *shoes* uses both hands.

- Both hands will begin in the letter S position. Close the fists with the thumb stretched in front of the fist. (Refer to the American Manual Alphabet in Chapter 18.)

- Hold the hands about shoulder width apart.

- Place hands at about mid-chest level.

Shoes: Part Two

- After forming the letter S with both hands, bring the two fists together.

- The fists tap each other and come away from each other again.

- Repeat this motion two times.

- Use this sign as you are getting dressed, as your child is getting dressed, or even as you see shoes in store windows.

are inside it is a good idea to let your child experiment with his feet without socks in a safe environment, where he is free from injury should he fall. If you put a shoe on baby, you are inhibiting her foot's ability to feel and grip the floor as she tries to balance.

Go ahead and put on the shoes when leaving the house to give adequate protection to those tiny toes. Shoes should be well fitted with only about $1/2$ inch of room to grow. Do not buy overly large shoes for baby to grow into, because it will cause your child to fall down.

Socks

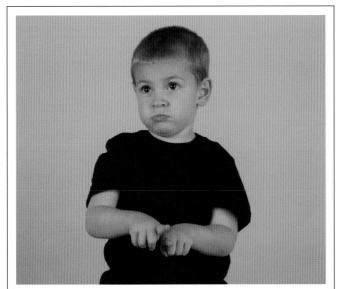

- The sign for *socks* uses both hands.

- Form the number 1 with both index fingers extended. (Refer to the number list in Chapter 19.)

- Point the hands downwards with the palms facing your body. The hands should be almost touching one another.

- Alternately move the fingers back and forth.

Hat

- *Hat* uses the dominant hand.

- Slightly tap the top of the head two times with the tips of your hand.

- Keep the palm flat and facing downward.

- *Hat*, because it is a simple sign, is very easy for baby to learn.

PLACES TO GO
Teaching baby signs replaces the grunt for these important places

We've all heard it: the emphatic "Uh, uh, uh" as your child points at something he desperately wants. It turns into a guessing game attempting to discern which object or place the baby is trying to talk about. It is so easy to get used to this method of communication and to respond by showing the variety of options of possible answers that parents forget there is a better way. First, encourage your child to say the

word by saying and signing the word yourself. After your child has tried to make an effort, whether it is verbal or through sign, then reward the child by giving him the object.

If your child isn't responding, help form his hands into the proper sign while saying the word out loud before giving him the coveted cracker or juice he is vying for. Don't overly frustrate the baby. If baby is frustrated then he is not going to

School

- *School* uses both hands.

- Hold the palms flat, straight, and facing one another.

- Clap hands together several times in a row to say *school*.

- Make the motion about two times. You can use this sign to describe your child's child-care center, enrichment classes, or when you attend a mother's day out.

Store

- *Store* uses both hands.

- Fold the hands with thumbs touching the folded four fingers.

- Place both hands in front of the face.

- Rotating from the wrist, move the hands upwards and then downwards several times.

be teachable. In those moments, perhaps give baby the first cracker, help him sign the word *cracker* while saying "Cracker," and then talk about the cracker—"Is that a yummy cracker? Mmmm, crackers are good!"

Your little one is a busy person on the go. As you take your baby to various destinations, teach him the signs. By having the signs in his vocabulary, your child won't have to resort to grunting and pointing and you won't have to guess what he wants. Here we will learn common places for baby: *school*, *store*, *church*, and *home*. As you read books about these places, as you drive to them, or arrive there, be sure to talk and sign.

If "church" is a little tricky, take your baby's lead. If he picks up just part of the sign, use it!

Church

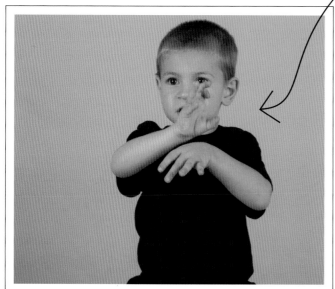

- *Church* uses both hands.

- Hold the stationary hand with the palm facing downward, fingers slightly bent.

- Form the letter C with the dominant hand. (Refer to the American Manual Alphabet in Chapter 18.)

- Place the letter C on top of the stationary hand.

Home

- *Home* uses the dominant hand.

- Fold the thumb and four fingers together. The fingers will be flat with no spaces between them.

- Place the hand on the side of the chin. Use the same side of the face as the hand you are signing with.

- Lift the hand off the chin and move it backward to touch and rest on the middle of the cheek.

SNACK TIME

Eating nutritious finger foods while using sign makes the most out of meal and snack time

Now that your baby's palate is a little more adapted to solid foods, have you begun to introduce a variety of finger foods? Finger foods help baby develop fine motor skills, while giving her the satisfaction of being able to self-feed and promoting independence. Here we will focus on the signs *orange*, *cheese*, *water*, and *juice*.

Finger foods should range in textures and in tastes. Try to help your child to not be a picky eater by exposing her to many different foods. If you've run out of creative, nutritious options, consider trying these less common finger food ideas with your baby (be sure to consult with your health care provider regarding age-appropriate snacks and bite sizes):

Orange

- *Orange* (the fruit) uses only one hand.

- Make an O shape with your dominant hand and place it in front of your mouth. (Refer to the American Manual Alphabet in Chapter 18.)

- Contract the O to a closed fist and then enlarge it back to normal size as though you have just squeezed an orange.

- The ASL sign for *orange* the fruit is different than orange the color, but for your baby they can be interchangeable.

Cheese

- *Cheese* uses both hands.

- Hands will be flat and pressed together.

- From the wrist twist the dominant palm outwards and then inwards several times. The stationary hand should stay flat.

Fruits:
Kiwi in bite size pieces
Blueberries
Avocado chunks (small)
Grapefruit chunks (small)

Veggies:
Tomato chunks
Cooked asparagus tips
Baked sweet potato fries
Cooked carrot chunks

Legumes:
Cooked edamame soy beans
  (not in pods)
Black beans
Chick peas
Hummus with bread or on
  a bagel
Bean burritos cut into bite-
  sized pieces

Cheese:
Shredded cheese
Grilled cheese bites

Mac and cheese
Cheese quesadilla bites

Meat/Fish/Protein:
Meatballs (cut into mini bites)
Hard-boiled eggs in pieces (over
  12 months)
Scrambled eggs (over
  12 months)
Salmon bites
Rotisserie chicken bites
Tuna salad mini sandwich bites
Egg salad mini sandwich bites

Veggie burger bites
Tofu chunks

Breads, Pastas, and Rice:
Whole-wheat toast sticks
Whole-wheat pancakes or
  waffles
Puffed rice snacks
Rice cooked in chicken broth
Whole-wheat bagel with smear
  of cream cheese
Rice cakes with cream cheese or
  100 percent fruit spread

Water

- *Water* uses one hand.

- Form the letter W with the index, middle, and ring finger extended. Keep the thumb and pinky closed. (Refer to the American Manual Alphabet in Chapter 18.)

- Bring the W to the bottom lip. Move the hand away from and to the lip again.

- Think of all the times you use or drink water with baby. Take advantage of the many opportunities to use this sign.

Juice

- *Juice* uses the dominant hand.

- Use the pinky finger to form a J-like motion starting at the bottom of the chin. (Refer to the American Manual Alphabet in Chapter 18.)

- The pinky finger starts at the chin and moves outward, making the dip of the letter J.

- Only the pinky finger is extended. All other fingers are closed into a fist.

LITTLE FRIENDS

Being around friends is good; make a play date for both parents and baby

Making a play date at the local park, your house, a friend's house, a mall's soft play area, or a local indoor playground is great for both parent and baby. It can help break up a long day for a stay-at-home mom or dad as well as provide a fun weekend activity for working parents, too! Connecting with other parents helps you understand that what you feel is normal, and gives you new ideas and tools with which to tackle similar issues. If you don't have a group to connect with, consider looking into your place of worship, Moms Offering Moms Support (MOMS) Clubs, or Mothers of Pre-schoolers (MOPS) International. These organizations will help you connect to other parents just like you.

Girl

Boy

- *Girl* uses the dominant hand.

- Begin with a closed fist with only the thumb extended.

- Place the thumb in the middle of the cheek. Use the cheek on the same side as the hand you are signing with.

- Move the thumb downward towards the chin.

- *Boy* uses the dominant hand.

- Imagine a boy's baseball cap on the head. The hand closes on the imaginary bill of the cap.

- The thumb and four fingers touch as you grab the bill of the cap.

- The palm faces downward.

As beneficial to parents as playgroups are, babies also benefit from the interaction with other children. While the baby is younger, solitary and onlooker play is normal. In a few months, the play will become more parallel and shared. Important concepts like taking turns and sharing are learned (though not always without a bite or a hit) during communal play. When shared play turns ugly, those moments present parents with teachable opportunities. Babies learn how to interact with each other through body movement and verbal cues. These early lessons help the baby later develop a better awareness of social interaction, including such concepts as body space, verbal cues, and eye contact.

Here we will learn the signs *girl*, *boy*, *friend*, and *play*. Use these signs before and after playgroup as you talk about going and after you leave. You can also use the signs during playgroup as you encourage your child to play nicely or to be a good friend.

Friend

- *Friend* uses both hands.

- Form the number 1 with both hands. Index fingers are extended; all other fingers are closed. (Refer to the number list in Chapter 19.)

- Begin by locking the two index fingers together.

- Next, alternate directions and lock the index fingers together again. Your child may modify this sign by simply touching the two index fingers together.

Play

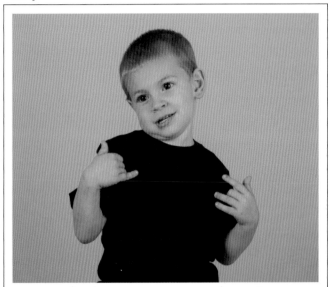

- *Play* uses both hands.

- Each hand forms the letter Y with the thumb and pinky finger extended. Keep all other fingers closed. (Refer to the American Manual Alphabet in Chapter 18.)

- Place hands at about chest level.

- Move the hands back and forth, rotating from the wrist.

ART TIME
Using colors, paper, and paints helps baby learn while having fun

If your baby is able to grasp a large, chunky crayon, then he is old enough to begin coloring. We're not talking masterpieces, but simple beginning scribbling. And it's an activity that can be done within the confines of a high chair, booster seat, or even a toddler table and chairs. Use large easy-to-grasp or triangular shaped crayons. Using crayons helps baby work on fine motor skills, teaches cause-and-effect, and develops

hand-eye coordination. If you are feeling brave enough, let baby paint. Painting doesn't have to be done with a paint-brush. If the baby isn't squeamish about different textures, experiment with edible "paints" such as sugar-free pudding, low-fat whipped cream, or tapioca. Put a little glob on your high chair or booster seat tray and let baby move the colors around. Unlike traditional paints, no worries if baby eats from

Crayons

- *Crayon* is a two-part gesture using two signs—*color* and *write*.

- *Color* uses the dominant hand in the number 5 position with all fingers extended. Place the hand in front of the lips and wiggle fingers back and forth with the palm facing the mouth.

- Next, sign *write* by using both hands. The stationary hand represents a tablet or paper.

- The dominant hand pretends to hold a crayon and write on the paper or stationary hand.

Paper

- *Paper* uses both hands.

- Hold the stationary hand with the palm facing upward.

- Hold the dominant hand flat. Brush the dominant hand over the stationary hand two times.

her hands, just consider it a snack! As baby gets a little older, encourage him to make shapes or letters with finger paints.

Here we will learn the signs *crayons*, *paper*, *paint*, and *messy.* Use these signs before and during the activity, and afterward as you are cleaning up the crafts. Before long baby will be asking through sign to color or paint.

Paint

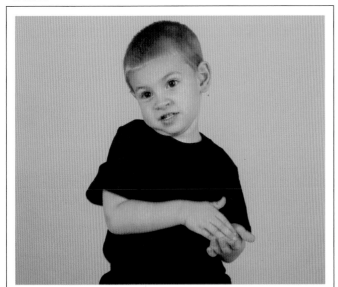

- *Paint* uses both hands.

- The stationary hand represents the wall or surface being painted. This hand is flat with palm facing upward.

- The dominant hand represents a paintbrush. Begin by brushing the back of the hand against the stationary hand upward.

- Next, brush the inside of the hand down the stationary hand.

- The sign should look as though your dominant hand is painting the stationary hand.

Messy

- *Mess* or *messy* uses both hands.

- Cup the hands with the fingers spread apart.

- Simultaneously rotate the hands in alternate directions.

CRAFT TIME
Grab some glue and create magnificent masterpieces with your toddler

Break out the glue and the smocks and prepare for a good ol' messy time helping your toddler learn. Not only do arts and crafts stimulate creativity, but they provide a great hands-on learning activity. Here we will learn *cut* or *scissors*, *glue*, *circle*, and *rectangle.* Use these signs while doing your own arts and crafts projects or try one of these fun ideas:

Cut out pictures of animals or interesting shapes from construction paper or magazines. Help baby glue those images on a piece of construction paper.

If you are a wine lover, make use of all the old corks collecting dust in a drawer. Using a dab of paint, help your child dip the end of the wine cork into the paint and then press the

Cut or Scissors

- *Cut* is a simple sign to learn.

- Using the dominant hand, form the number 2 with your index and middle fingers extended and the rest closed. Point the fingertips straight out as though they were scissors.

- Move the two fingers together and apart in a cutting motion and simultaneously move the hand forward as though cutting through a piece of paper.

Glue

The sign shown here isn't exact (pinky shouldn't be extended), but it's okay for your child to create his own variation as long as it's clear and consistent!

- *Glue* uses the dominant hand.

- Form the G shape with the dominant hand. G is formed using the index and thumb extended with all other fingers closed. (Refer to the American Manual Alphabet in Chapter 18.)

- Hold the hand in front of your body just above the opposite (non-signing hand) shoulder.

- While closing the index finger and thumb together repeatedly, move the hand across until it is even with the signing hand shoulder.

cork onto the paper. Your child can make random designs, or with your help, can make shapes, smiley faces, or even an animal.

Tired of being indoors? Go outside with a cheap bottle of bubbles and add a few drops of food coloring. Pop the bubbles on a piece of paper and see the cool designs emerge.

Have your child lie down on a large piece of white banner paper and trace his outline. Have him decorate it with crayons, glued-on pasta pieces or goldfish, or paint.

Decorate your driveway or sidewalk with sidewalk chalk. If you want a clean slate for tomorrow, simply wash off the chalk or wait for a rainy day.

Circle

- *Circle* uses one or both hands.

- Begin with hand or hands forming the number 1. Keep all other fingers closed.

- Touch the tips of the index fingers to each other. Next, move fingers away from each other, each drawing half a circle that meets at the bottom, forming a whole.

- Or, using one hand, draw a circle shape with the index finger.

Rectangle

- *Rectangle* uses both hands.

- Much like the sign for *circle*, you will draw the shape of a rectangle with both hands.

- Once again, form the number 1 with both hands. Begin with both fingers touching.

- Move the fingers apart sideways, downward, and then sideways again until they meet after forming a full rectangle.

PLAYTIME PREPOSITIONS
Fun games to help you play with baby and avoid the TV trap

Although it might seem harmless, turning on the tube even once a day for a child under three years old can have detrimental effects. A baby or toddler who is consistently entertained by the television learns that something else is able to entertain baby, not himself any longer. Instead of playing and learning with toys, animals, books, or a caregiver, your child's time has been wasted. Though sticking in a baby DVD is a temptation we've all indulged in at one time or another, try to resist. Use the time to practice more signs and help engage baby through games. Recruit a sibling or older child as well and you'll help strengthen familial bonds while gaining a few minutes for yourself!

Great activities for a child from 12 to 18 months include: Peek-a-boo

In

- *In* uses both hands. The motion demonstrates the action of something going inside an object.

- Begin with the stationary hand forming the letter C. (Refer to the American Manual Alphabet in Chapter 18.)

- Fold the thumb and four fingers of the dominant hand together.

- Place the dominant hand inside the stationary letter C.

Out

- *Out* uses both hands.

- The stationary hand is flat with the palm facing downward.

- Fold the thumb and four fingers of the dominant

hand together while moving the hand and arm backward away from the stationary hand.

- This motion represents something leaving or going out.

Popping bubbles
Crawling chase
Rolling the ball back and forth
Setting up boxes and pillows to go through, under, and over
Having a designated baby cabinet in the kitchen full of pans, pots, and spoons with which baby can safely play. Throw a few pieces of cereal in the pan for baby to "cook."
Too many toys? Periodically box up the toys that baby is not interested in. In a month or two, bring the box back out and box up the ones that were out previously. The old toys

inside the box will be like a new treasure.
Buy a cheap set of nesting cups. Show baby how to stack and let baby knock over the cup tower.
Here we will learn the signs *in*, *out*, *under*, and *over,* which can be used in many of these baby games.

Under

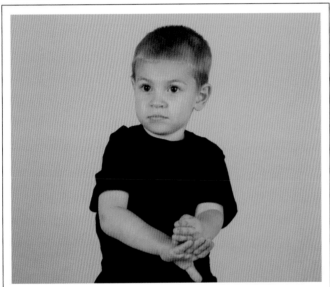

- *Under* uses both hands.
- The stationary hand can either be flat or vertical.
- Using either an open palm or a closed fist, move the dominant hand underneath the stationary hand.
- The motion represents something moving or being underneath another object.

Over

- *Over* uses both hands.
- Hold each hand straight and flat with all fingers extended and together and the thumb pressed in.
- Place the stationary hand sideways so that the pinky finger is facing the floor.
- Move the dominant hand flat over the stationary hand, demonstrating an object going over something else.

CHARACTER TRAITS
Instill positive traits through living a life of character

One of the greatest fulfillments of parenting is seeing your child be kind or generous, empathetic, caring, and trustworthy. Here we will learn the signs *kind, mean, brave* and *strong*. But beyond just words of instruction and caution, these traits are taught through active parenting. A child learns kindness by watching mom or dad extend kindness. A child learns how to respect his peers, teachers, and parents through watching his parents' interactions with each other, with their children, and with their peers. What character traits do you want to instill?

Thankfulness is a trait that seems to be evaporating from modern-day culture. In our microwave, instant-gratification society, appreciation and gratitude have often been forgotten. Instill thankfulness by talking about the things in your life

Kind

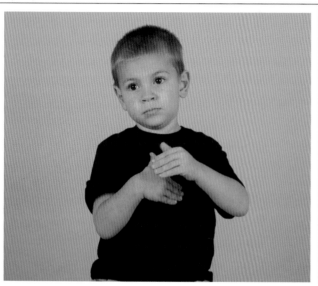

- *Kind* uses both hands.

- Place the stationary hand palm facing the ground, with the hand slightly cupped.

- Gently stroke the top of the hand with the dominant hand.

- To further convey the meaning of the word, say the word "Kind" with a sweet tone and with a sweet expression on your face.

Mean

- *Mean* uses both hands.

- Begin with both hands in a loose cup. Place one hand near the chin area, while the other hand is at chest level.

- Bring both hands together quickly, brushing one hand against the other. As they brush, close the fingers together.

- The sign will end with both hands apart, in opposite positions from where each hand began.

- Be sure your expression and tone of voice look and sound mean.

you are grateful for—health, shelter, all of the little blessings that are a part of your life. Point out what you do have and are grateful for, and choose not to focus on what you don't have—especially in front of your child.

Teach trustworthiness by being a parent of your word. If you tell your child you are going to do something, make every effort to actually do it. If you commit to an obligation, demonstrate follow-through by completing it and not backing out.

Integrity is often described as how you behave when no one else is looking. With kids at home, somebody is always looking, observing and noticing. Who are you all the time? Are you a person of integrity?

Brave

- *Brave* uses both hands.

- Both hands begin at shoulder level, slightly cupped and open.

- Next, move the hands toward each shoulder.

- Close the hands into a fist as both hands pull away from the shoulders simultaneously.

Strong

- *Strong* can use either one or both hands and arms.

- Flex your arm as though you are making a muscle.

- Don't be afraid to emphasize your tone and expression to help convey the meaning of *strong*.

71

KNOWING THE ANSWER

How much? Are you sure? Expanding questions and answers

Emerging toddlers seem to be gifted with the ability to understand and say "No." In fact, rarely do we see such pleasure as that experienced by a child who has learned to say "No." The word falls off her lips with a sparkle in her eye. She enjoys the exercise in power, the response it tends to elicit from the parent, and the beginnings of independence. While *yes* and *no* are basic answers, here we will help your toddler begin to learn more words than *yes* and *no,* with **much, never, not,** and **sure.** Expanding vocabulary means enhancing communication.

Using inflection and animation with these signs will also help convey the meaning of the words. Don't be afraid to exaggerate *much* or *never.* The exaggeration makes the words more interesting to the child, helps give conceptual understanding, and drives home the point.

Much

- *Much* uses both hands.

- Hold both hands slightly cupped with the fingers apart and slightly bent.

- Begin with the fingertips of each hand facing and touching one another.

- Pull the hands away from one another, turning the palms slightly upward.

Never

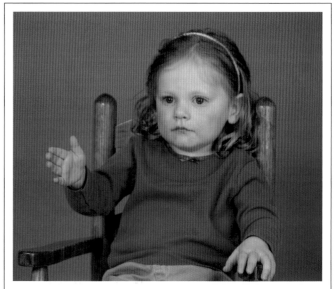

- *Never* uses the dominant hand.

- Begin by making the letter B. Press the thumb against the palm with the remaining four fingers extended with no spaces between

them. (Refer to the American Manual Alphabet in Chapter 18.)

- Start the motion at about head level. Make a zig-zag motion downward with the hand.

One time when you may have seen your toddler say "No" quite a bit is when you leave her. Despite the way your child may cling to you like a monkey on a tree, or cry and carry on as though the caregiver is intent on torture, your child's separation anxiety is normal. And, more than likely, only a few moments after mom and dad head out the door, your child has settled down.

Whatever you do, don't let your child's separation anxiety prevent you from going out. Having some alone time without your child is an important part of reconnection between you and your spouse. You need moments together that do not revolve around baby. Separation also teaches your child that when you leave, you will come back.

Not

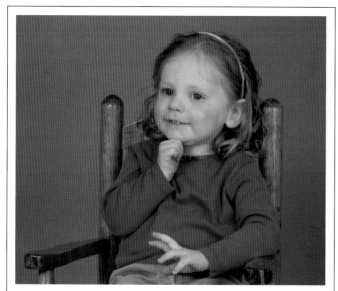

Sure

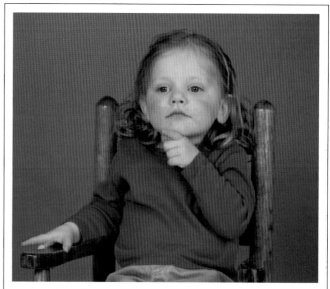

- *Not* is a simple sign using the dominant hand.

- Begin by forming a fist with the thumb facing upward.

- Place the inside of the tip of the thumb behind the chin.

- Flick the thumb forward away from the chin.

- Place the dominant index finger on the lips.

- Move the index finger away from the lips in a downward direction.

- The sign will end with the index finger pointing outwards.

- In ASL, this sign can also mean *true* or *absolutely*.

QUESTIONS
Equip your child with the questions to learn more about his world

Questions are integral to how your toddler will learn about the world around him. Though parents may grow weary of hearing "Why?" yet again, asking these probing questions is a fundamental process of learning. By teaching your child signs for questions, you will provide him with the ability to ask questions wherever he is, in any setting. Having the ability to sign allows him to ask questions even in quiet environments

when normally he wouldn't be allowed to speak. If the response is too long, respond back with the sign for *later*.

Later is made by placing the thumb of the letter L on the center of the sideways, stationary palm. Twist the L downwards, pivoting from the thumb, while keeping the stationary hand still. (Refer to the American Manual Alphabet in Chapter 18.)

KNACK BABY SIGN LANGUAGE

Why

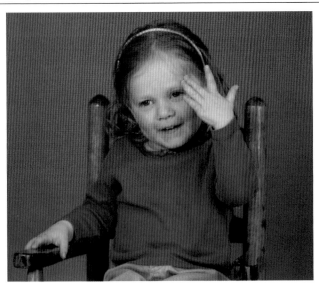

- *Why* uses the dominant hand.

- Place the palm of the hand at the forehead, touching the forehead with the middle finger.

- Pull the hand away from the forehead with the fingers slightly bent.

- Be sure your tone and expression are reflecting this question.

Where

- *Where* is a one-handed sign. You will use your dominant hand.

- Extend the index finger out, keeping all other fingers in a closed fist.

- Move your index finger back and forth by shifting your wrist to the left and then to the right several times.

- Have a questioning look on your face. Speak or mouth the word "Where?" as you sign.

As you teach your child the signs, be sure to look expressive, allowing your face to reflect the question being asked. The facial and body language help relate to the child what the question means. Your voice should sound captivating too. Your child's interest will dwindle if the signs are presented in a boring or lifeless tone. Give life to the signs through voice inflection.

Feel free to repeat the sign while speaking it several times for effective understanding.

GREEN ● LIGHT

You're probably comfortable signing at home in your own surroundings without the watching eyes of passersby. But, are you comfortable when you are at a restaurant or at the mall? Don't worry about drawing attention to yourself. Remember, consistent signing is crucial to success, so use your signs in every setting.

What

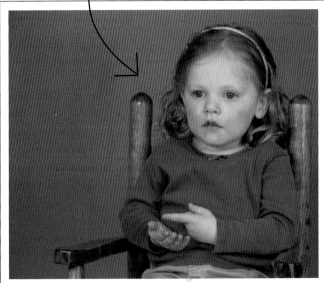

- *What* uses both hands.

- Strike the index finger of your dominant hand quickly against the open palm of the stationary hand.

- Your eyes and face should look somewhat confused.

Who

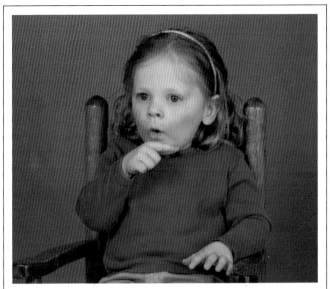

- *Who* uses the dominant hand.

- Place the index finger 1 to 2 inches away from the mouth.

- Next, circle the index finger around the mouth about two times.

- Remember that the tone of your voice will help your child understand the question being asked.

MOVING AROUND

Whether inside or out, get moving for fun entertainment and physical activity

Now that your toddler is mobile having signs to describe the constant array of movement is going to benefit both you and baby. Here we will learn the signs *crawl, sit, walk,* and *run.* Keeping your toddler busy with physical activity is good for both parent and child. First, it gives your toddler a way to burn off some of that never ending energy supply. Second,

it helps your child learn what he is capable of and to experiment with new movement. It also stimulates creative thinking. Whether inside or out, getting physical is fun and free!
Ideas for indoor play:
Turn on the radio or play your favorite CD and dance to the music.

Crawl

- "Crawl" uses both hands.

- Hold both hands with palms facing up. The stationary hand is flat, representing the floor or surface a child crawls on.

- The dominant hand forms the letter U with the index and middle fingers extended. (Refer to the American Manual Alphabet in Chapter 18.) Place the U on the stationary hand, palm up.

- Move the dominant hand across the hand while simultaneously wiggling the index and middle finger. These fingers stay together and have no space between them.

Sit

- *Sit* uses both hands.

- Form the letter H with both hands. H uses the index and middle finger extended and pressed against each other. (Refer to the American Manual Alphabet in Chapter 18.)

- The stationary palm faces downward and the hand is flat.

- Rest the dominant fingers on top of the stationary fingers. Move the dominant hand on and off two times.

Get down on your hands and knees and play chase while crawling.

Using blankets and pillows, create a safe and soft obstacle course for your child to crawl over and dive through.

Play hide and seek.

Use laundry baskets as make-believe boats. Push your child around the floor in an exciting deep-sea adventure. Afterwards, have your child take her favorite animals on a voyage.

Ideas for outdoor play:

Play chase with your child or enlist siblings or other friends for a game of freeze tag.

Kick a ball back and forth. Not only is this fun, but it teaches cause and effect.

Throw or roll a ball back and forth.

Take a child-led walk and let your child decide (within reason) where to go.

Here are some useful words for helping your baby describe what he likes to do.

Walk

- *Walk* uses both hands.

- Each hand is flat, palm facing downward with all fingers extended and together.

- Alternately move each hand back and forth. The motion should look like steps being taken.

- The alternating motion of the hands should not be hurried, but in a slow walking pace.

Run

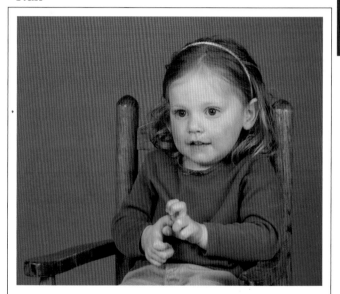

- *Run* uses both hands.

- Place the dominant hand close to the body with the index and middle finger pointed outwards.

- Next, wrap the other hand's index finger around the dominant hand thumb.

- Move both hands forward quickly, still joined together outwards and away from your body.

POTTY TRAINING
Making the transition from diapers to big-boy or big-girl pants

When is the best time to potty train? Only you and your child can answer that question. While most children are potty trained between 18 months and three years old, there are a few who choose to push the limit a little longer. Rest assured that no matter how impossible it may seem, your child will not be going to kindergarten in a diaper. Eventually, the desire to use the toilet will come. You can begin to sense your child might be ready for toilet training when:

Your child is able to stay dry for at least two hours at a time.

Your child has regular bowel movements.

Your child begins to ask for big-boy or big-girl underpants or panties.

Bathroom or Toilet

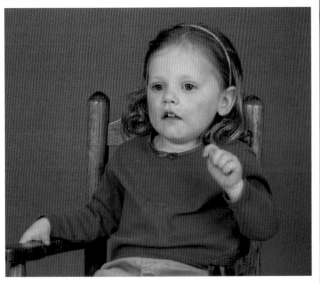

- *Bathroom* or *toilet* uses the dominant hand.

- Form the letter T. Rest the thumb in between the closed index and middle finger. (Refer to the American Manual Alphabet in Chapter 18.)

- Move the hand back and forth from the wrist.

Stand

- *Stand* uses both hands.

- Hold the stationary hand flat, palm facing upwards.

- With the dominant hand, form the number 2 with index and middle fingers extended. (Refer to the number list in Chapter 19.)

- Place the tips of the fingers on top of the stationary hand, representing a standing position.

Your child begins to tell you when he or she needs to be changed.

Your child is willing and able to obey simple commands.

Whatever method you decide to use to train your child, keep in mind that you should avoid training during stressful times for your child. If Mom is returning to work, or if your child is changing child-care centers, it is not the time to introduce potty training. If you are moving or expecting a new baby, avoid training until your child has adjusted to the new move or child. Once training, don't penalize or criticize your child for accidents. Reinforce potty successes with praise. And use the following signs—*bathroom, stand, down,* and *turn on*—to give your child more ways to communicate when he needs to go.

Use this sign when you put the toilet seat down.

Down

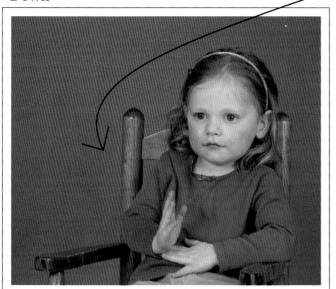

- *Down* uses both hands.

- Place the stationary hand at about chest level. Hold the hand with the palm facing the ground with all fingers extended and together.

- Place the dominant hand so that the palm of the hand is next to the fingertips of the stationary hand.

- Slowly rest the dominant hand down on top of the stationary hand.

Turn On (the Faucet)

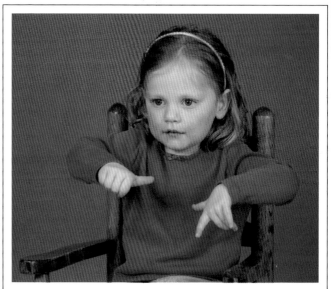

- Place both hands over imaginary bathroom faucet knobs.

- Twist each hand simultaneously towards one another as though you are turning on the water.

- To say *turn off*, move the hands back in opposite directions as though you are turning off the faucet.

SAFETY WORDS

Accidents can be avoided with proactive cautionary measures and simple common sense

As the parent of your child, you are ultimately responsible for her safety at all times. Be sure to take the necessary precautions to prevent accidents and use the signs shown here—*go*, *help*, *lost*, and *slow*—to help keep track of your child when at the park, in the house, or anywhere you are out and about with your child. Remember these basic safety measures:

Keep doors locked and closed at all times. If your child has figured out how to unlock the door, then it is time for an additional lock. Open doors can allow curious bodies to get outside.

Never let your child play outside without supervision, even for just a minute. Accidents and accidental drowning can

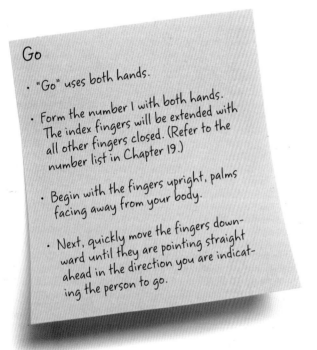

Go

- "Go" uses both hands.

- Form the number 1 with both hands. The index fingers will be extended with all other fingers closed. (Refer to the number list in Chapter 19.)

- Begin with the fingers upright, palms facing away from your body.

- Next, quickly move the fingers downward until they are pointing straight ahead in the direction you are indicating the person to go.

Help

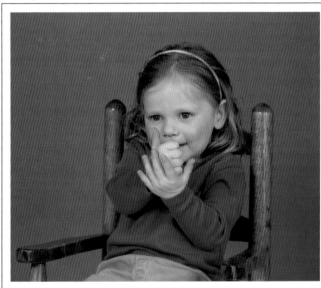

- *Help* uses both hands.

- The dominant hand will form a closed fist.

- The stationary hand is flat, palm facing upward. Place this hand directly underneath the dominant fist.

- Raise both hands simultaneously as though the bottom hand is helping the top hand to move.

occur quickly. Even running inside to answer a quick telephone call or to check on laundry can lead to a serious accident. Toddlers can drown in something as inconspicuous as a container filled with rainwater.

Chemicals and medications should be well out of reach of your child. Medicine should be kept in childproof containers and put away.

While cooking, make sure pot and pan handles are turned toward the back of the counter. Little hands can easily reach up, grabbing and pulling a hot pan or pot onto the child.

Bolt and secure furniture pieces, such as bookcases or television console units, to the wall. Toddlers love to climb, and these heavy pieces, if not secured, can fall onto their bodies.

Routinely clean toys and throw away broken ones. Pieces that break off can be potential choking hazards. Additionally, keeping toys clean and in good condition encourages proper play and use of the toy.

Lost

- *Lost* uses both hands.

- Begin the motion as though you are making the *more* sign with the tips of the fingers touching.

- Next, turn both palms facing downward as the fingers relax and come apart.

- This motion should look like something just slipped away, or was lost or dropped.

Slow

- *Slow* uses both hands.

- Both hands are flat, palms facing downward.

- Slide dominant hand from the fingertips toward the wrist of the stationary hand.

- This motion should not be made too quickly, and should be representative of the word *slow*.

81

BEDTIME
When baby starts to wake up at night . . . again

Here we will learn the signs *night-night*, *dreams*, and *I love you*, all great words for the nighttime routine. Routines are a great way to cue your child about what is going to come next. When your child has an expectation and isn't guessing when bedtime is, he will have less anxiety and will feel calmer and more relaxed.

Nothing is more frustrating than for a parent to finally achieve sleeping through the night, only for the child to begin waking up again. If baby suddenly begins nighttime waking, there is a reason for this sleeping pattern disruption.

Ear infections are a common culprit. Because the pain is more acute while the child is lying down, it is often during sleep that the infection may cause pain for the baby. Little clues, like the baby pulling on an ear or crying when horizontal,

Night-Night

- *Night-night* uses both arms and hands.

- Hold your stationary arm bent in front of you, as though your arm were in a sling.

- Bend the dominant hand at the knuckles.

- Cross the palm over the stationary forearm two times. The palm will be facing the body.

Dreams: Part One

- *Dreams* uses one hand only.

- The dominant hand forms the letter X using a bent index finger at both joints. All other fingers are closed. (Refer to the American Manual Alphabet in Chapter 18.)

- Place the tip of the index finger near your temple. Use the same side of your head as the hand with which you are signing.

may help you recognize an ear infection. It is always a good idea to check with the pediatrician's office to rule out an ear infection after a night or two of nighttime waking.

Emerging molars and the pain from cutting teeth also may be waking your child. Consult your doctor for his or her preferred over-the-counter pain reliever for your child.

Too many naps or too long of a nap may also be the cause. Consider reducing naptime or eliminating a nap if it is interfering with nighttime sleep.

Last, baby might be having a bout of separation anxiety. Use a security object at bedtime by talking about and putting one with baby at night. While it is okay to talk, sing, or pat baby, resist the urge to pick baby up or lie down with baby. Doing those two things will undermine your baby's ability to fall asleep independently.

Dreams: Part Two

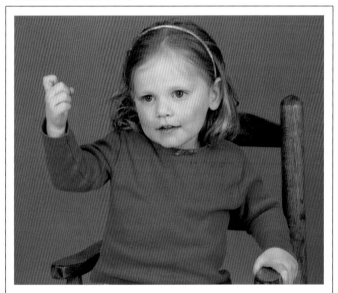

- After placing the finger near the temple, wiggle the finger while moving it in an outward direction away from your head.

- Your facial expression should look as though you are dreaming.

- Make sure your tone sounds calming as you sign and say, "Sweet dreams."

- Use this sign as you wish your child sweet dreams at naptime, bedtime, or while reading a story that describes a bedtime routine.

I Love You

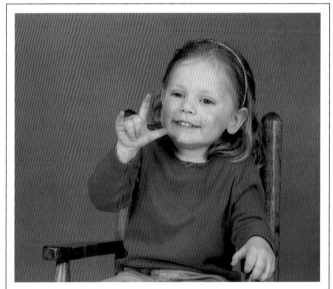

- *I love you* can be said with just one hand.

- Extend the thumb, index finger, and pinky finger. The third and fourth fingers are closed.

- Face the palm outward.

- *I love you* can be used throughout the day, through a window, or as a car is pulling away.

OUTDOOR FUN
Give your toddler a day of adventure with a trip to the park

Going to the park allows your child an opportunity to be adventurous and promotes good physical activity. It is also free, fun, and good for both parent and baby. Here we will learn the signs *swing*, *outside*, *bicycle*, and *see-saw*.

Before you head out the door, take a moment to consider the park you are visiting.

Is the surface safe? Chances are at some point your little one is going to take a tumble. By going to a park that has a good, cushiony surface such as solid foam, wood chips, or pea gravel, you may help prevent an emergency room visit. Avoid parks that only have grass—which doesn't have much give—or concrete surfaces.

Is the equipment age- and developmentally appropriate? Look for a park that has playground equipment specifically

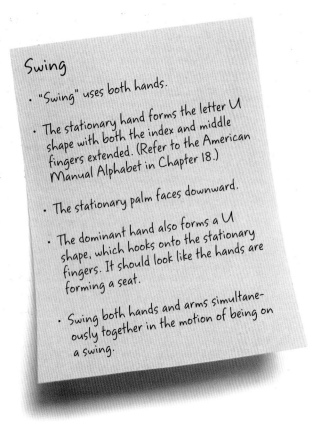

Swing

- "Swing" uses both hands.
- The stationary hand forms the letter U shape with both the index and middle fingers extended. (Refer to the American Manual Alphabet in Chapter 18.)
- The stationary palm faces downward.
- The dominant hand also forms a U shape, which hooks onto the stationary fingers. It should look like the hands are forming a seat.
- Swing both hands and arms simultaneously together in the motion of being on a swing.

Outside

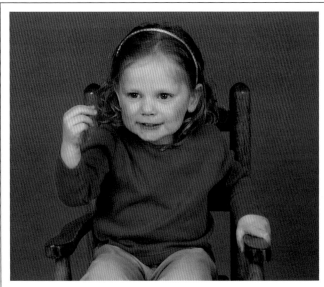

- *Outside* uses one hand.
- Begin with the dominant hand slightly open and cupped.
- Pull the hand in a backward direction while simultaneously closing the fingers together.
- Repeat this motion quickly to say *outside* rather than simply saying *out*.

geared toward little ones. Watch for any potential areas where your toddler could fall through.

Go over your expectations and park rules before heading to the park, and enforce them while you are there. Swing rules might include: Avoid walking in front of or behind a swing; no twisting; and no pushing an empty swing. On the slide, remind your toddler it is for going down only. Encourage your toddler to stay away from the perimeter of the park to prevent stranger danger, road drop-offs, or even unintentional wandering to discover something in the adjoining yard or area.

Last, have fun. If you plan to stay a while, pack sunscreen, snacks, water, or even a picnic lunch. Enjoy this outdoor adventure.

Bicycle

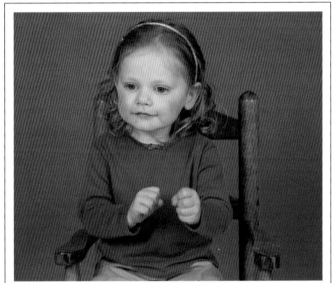

- *Bicycle* uses both hands.

- Form closed fists in the letter S position with the thumbs resting in front of the closed fingers of the fists.

- Place one fist slightly above the other first.

- Move both hands simultaneously in a circular motion as though pumping the pedals of a bike.

See-Saw

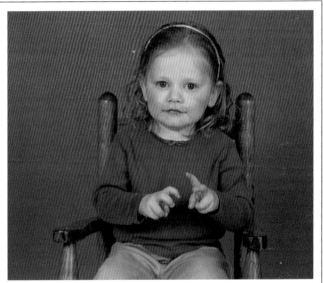

- Form a curved number 2 with each hand at chest level, hands facing one another.

- Place one hand slightly higher than the other.

- Simultaneously move the higher hand down and the lower hand up in a see-saw motion. Repeat.

GROUP PLAY
Teach your toddler the signs and skills to share during play

The concept of sharing is a tough one to swallow for any toddler. What toddler willingly wants to let someone else play with her special toys at home or at school? Sharing is a concept that needs to be learned; rarely does one share without having been taught to do so. Here we will learn the signs *share*, *blocks*, *build*, and *together*. Use these signs as your child plays. Not only will you equip him with signs to

communicate, but you'll also encourage social sharing skills.

If your toddler is having difficulties learning to share, try these suggestions:

When a friend is coming over to play, allow your child to pick out two or three of his most precious toys to put away. This way you are giving your child some control and input in the situation and will help him feel less threatened

Share

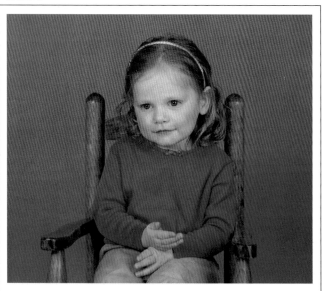

- *Share* uses both hands.

- The stationary palm faces upwards and is flat.

- Place the dominant palm sideways on top of the stationary palm.

- Move the palm back and forth in a slight sweeping motion.

Blocks

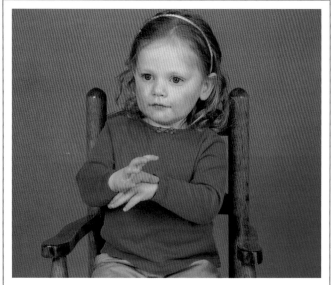

- *Blocks* can use one or both hands.

- Form half a square with a loose letter C shape to represent the block. As an alternative, form a square

- or cube shape using both hands.

- Move the hands or hand as though you are placing blocks next to one another or in a circle.

by sharing his most treasured possessions. Be consistent. Always expect your child to share. Don't allow certain times or items to be off-limits because it sends a confusing message.

Any time your child shares anything, from offering you a bite of his meal to letting a sibling touch or play with a toy, use praise. This positive reinforcement will help your toddler associate sharing as a positive, not negative act.

Create sharing opportunities. For example, if you are hosting playgroup, give your child a special snack to pass out to each child. Let her witness the pleasure sharing brings to other people.

Emphasize taking turns. If your child really wants an object, remind her that her turn is coming soon, and then make sure it does.

Last, talk about and model sharing in your own life. Live a life of example.

Build

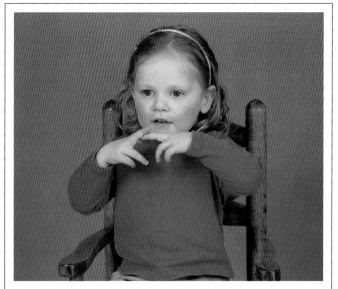

- *Build* uses both hands.

- Both hands are flat, palms facing downwards.

- Begin with one hand underneath the other. Next, bring the bottom hand on top. Continue this pattern.

- This motion should move upwards as though you are building something.

Together

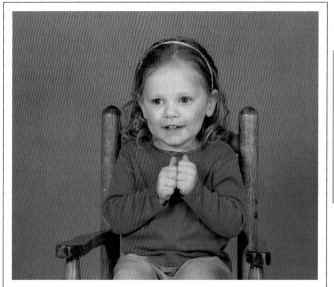

- *Together* uses both hands.

- Form the letter A with both hands by making a closed fist with the thumb pressed to the side.

- Place both hands together, with the thumbs on top.

- Simultaneously move both hands together in a circular motion.

- Make sure the hands remain in a horizontal position as you make the circular motion.

WORK & PLAY

Assess your 18-month-old's verbal and cognitive development skills

As your child approaches 18 months old, you'll begin to notice that your baby, well, doesn't look like much of a baby anymore. He has probably begun to lose his babyish appearance, thinning out a bit, and has definitely begun to act more like a child than a baby. Here are some signs for your growing toddler's playtime: *hammer*, *work*, *sword*, and *battle*.

While your child is growing more independent, careful supervision of your child may be more important now than ever. Everything inside and out is a new adventure. Be sure that you have taken all necessary precautions to make your home a safe sanctuary for your baby.

Prepare for your next doctor visit with a review of typical milestones for 18-month-olds. It is important to communicate with your doctor if your child is not reaching these milestones.

Hammer

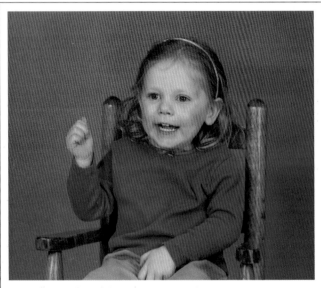

- *Hammer* uses both hands.

- The stationary palm is slightly bent, facing upward.

- The dominant hand looks as though it is grasping a hammer.

- The dominant hand makes the motion of hammering onto the stationary hand.

Work

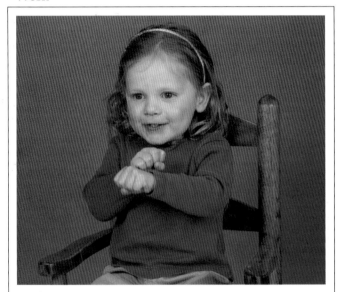

- *Work* uses both hands.

- Each hand forms a closed fist.

- Knock the dominant fist on top of the wrist of the stationary hand.

- Repeat this motion several times.

18-month milestone check

Physical:

Child is able to run.

Child can begin to undress.

Child can feed himself with a spoon.

Cognitive:

Your child will probably be able to say his name (or close to it!)

Child has a vocabulary of around 20 words and begins to use words in two-word phrases.

Child uses tone as much as the words themselves to indicate meaning.

Child is able to identify body parts (i.e. head, nose, or eye) by pointing.

Sword

- *Sword* uses both hands.

- The sign looks as though you are drawing a sword out of a holster.

- Begin the motion with the dominant hand reaching into the stationary hand. The stationary hand is cupped around an imaginary holster.

- Next, the dominant hand and arm pull the sword out.

Battle

- *Battle* uses both hands.

- Both hands have slightly bent palms with the fingers spread apart.

- The palms are turned toward the body, with the tip of each hand facing the other.

- Move the hands sideways, first to the right, then to the left. Repeat. This back-and-forth motion mimics battling back and forth.

DRESS-UP FUN

While playing dress-up, listen to your toddler talk

Playtime is a good opportunity to listen to how your child's verbal skills are progressing. Every toddler will mispronounce some words and have some letter or sound substitutions. It's natural to worry about whether your child is achieving age-appropriate verbal skills. No toddler speaks perfectly. If your child shows the following speech quirks, don't be alarmed. Age-appropriate sound and speech patterns include:

Substituting the *f* or *d* sound for the *th* sound.
Substituting the *w* sound for the *r* sound.
Omitting final consonant sounds.
Being understood primarily by parent.
Reversing sounds in a word.
Generalization of words (i.e. *dada* may mean all men, *cat* may mean all animals).

Pretty

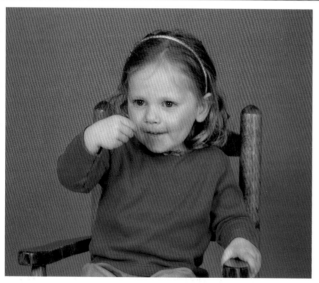

- *Pretty* is formed using the dominant hand.

- First, begin with the fingers spread apart, slightly bent.

- Circle the hand around the face.

- As you end the circle, draw the fingers together and pull them away from the face.

Barrette

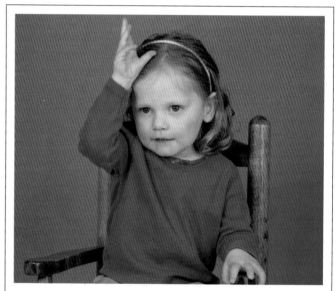

- *Barrette* uses the dominant hand.

- Form the letter G with index finger and thumb extended and all other fingers closed. (Refer to the American Manual Alphabet in Chapter 18.)

- Using the same side of the head as the hand you are signing with place the fingers near the top of the side of the head. Collapse the index finger onto the thumb as though fastening a barrette.

Understanding more than the child is able to verbally communicate.

Even though your child is beginning to talk, keep signing with him. The use of signs helps your child understand concepts and meanings of words and phrases. Complex sounds are never an issue with sign. Incorporating sign language as part of the daily routine will only continue to enhance your child's blossoming language and speech development.

• • • • • • • • • • • • • RED ● LIGHT • • • • • • • • • • • • •

By three years of age, your child should be understood easily by others. Your child should also be making long sentences with five or more words and incorporating the use of the word "and." Seeking a speech pathology evaluation is always a good idea if your three-year-old is not yet doing this. Speech and language acquisition are vital stepping stones for reading later, and the sooner the issues are addressed, the easier they are corrected.

Lipstick

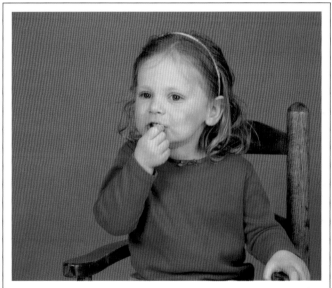

- *Lipstick* uses the dominant hand.

- Pretend to hold a tube of lipstick.

- Next, pretend to apply the lipstick on your lips.

- Use this sign with your child's toy lipstick or a stick of lip balm.

- Many ASL signs, like lipstick, are iconic.

Purse

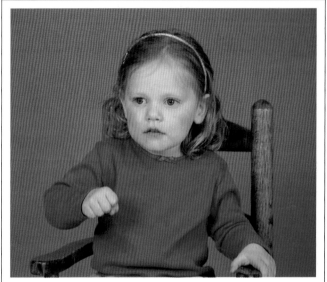

- *Purse* uses one hand.

- Pretend to grasp the handle of a purse with the dominant hand.

- Slightly move the hand up and down as though you are about to take the purse and go.

IMAGINARY PLAY
Creative learning through dress-up play helps stimulate the imagination

Putting on a costume or dress-up clothes is a powerful creative tool for your toddler. Suddenly, your child has the ability to morph from a young child to anybody he wants to be. Through a simple wardrobe change, your child can become a superhero, a fireman, a princess, or even a dragon. Encourage creative imaginary play in your child by having a wide repertoire of dress-up clothes. Have a large drawer, chest, or plastic tub designated for dress-up clothes that your child can access easily for play and cleaning up afterwards. If the box or drawer is overflowing, consider rotating out the selection. Not only will it be easier to find costumes, but rotation will make old costumes seem new again.

Policeman

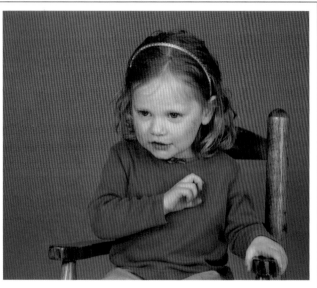

- *Policeman* uses the dominant hand.

- Curve the index finger and thumb as though they are holding a police badge.

- Place the fingers on the shoulder area where you would see a police badge on an officer.

Fireman

- *Fireman* uses the dominant hand.

- Place the hand on the top of the forehead with the palm facing outwards.

- The hand should look like the top of the fireman's helmet.

Creating a dress-up wardrobe doesn't have to break the budget. Visit Goodwill or other secondhand thrift shops for inexpensive additions to the dress-up drawer. Hit the Halloween stores on November 1 to get great deals on all the leftover costumes. Call upon cousins or siblings for dance recital costumes or old sports jerseys to add to the collection. Keep some clips handy to clip the clothes to fit to avoid tripping and falling on loose fabric.

While your child is playing dress-up, take the opportunity to hone her fine motor skills. Help her use Velcro, zippers, and buttons and tie string or ribbons. Practicing on dress-up clothes will make it easier to learn how to use these items when they are older.

Dressing up can also be used to reassure your child. If she is about to go to the doctor or hospital for a series of tests, take advantage of the opportunity to act out what might happen at the doctor's office to reduce anxiety and fear.

Princess

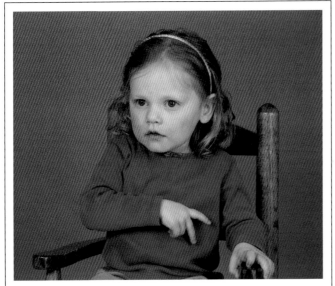

- *Princess* uses the dominant hand.

- Form the letter P using the middle and index fingers spread apart with the thumb placed snugly in between. The pinky and ring finger are closed. (Refer to the American Manual Alphabet in Chapter 18.)

- Place the P on the opposite shoulder of the hand signing.

- Lift the P off the shoulder and move it in an arc-like shape, until the P rests on the opposite hip.

Ballerina or Dancer

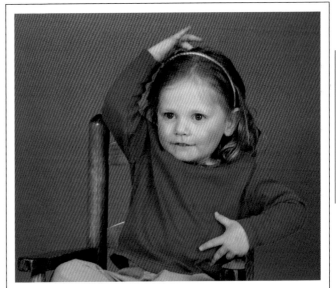

- *Ballerina* or *dancer* is made with both hands.

- Place one hand on the top of the head, and place the other hand on the side of the waist, much like a ballerina might stand.

- Or, make a sign similar to *stand*, with the number 2 standing on the stationary flat palm. Glide the fingertips on the top of the stationary palm back and forth as though they were dancing.

MUSICAL EXPERIMENTATION

Music helps your child express himself, and promotes creative use of mind and body

Having and creating musical instruments for your child to play with helps stimulate cognitive development and sensory awareness. In addition to expressing himself through sign and through words, your child can learn the power of expressing himself through sound. Using basic songs like the ABCs helps develop speech and language skills, as well as honing memory and recall ability.

Keep musical instruments grouped together and easily accessible. Encourage experimentation with a variety of sounds using household objects such as pans, boxes, a paper towel tube filled with beans, or a coffee can with rocks. Pique creativity while encouraging musical awareness. If possible,

Piano

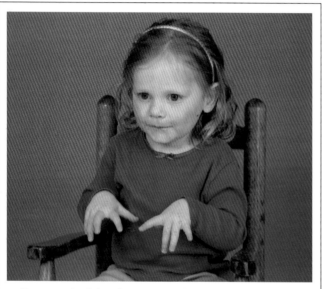

- *Piano* uses both hands.

- Simply move the fingers back and forth as though they were playing the keys on a piano.

- If possible, show and play an actual piano to your child when making the sign so the child understands the association of the sign.

Bell

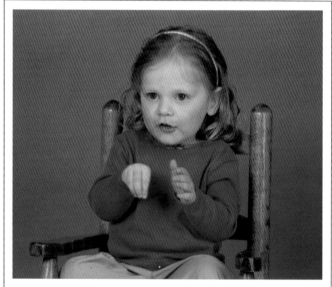

- *Bell* uses both hands.

- The stationary hand is flat and sideways with the palm facing the other hand.

- The dominant hand is pretending to hold a bell between the index finger and thumb. The other three fingers are extended straight.

- Lightly strike the dominant hand into the stationary hand as though you are ringing a bell.

record your child's musical creations. Playing back his compositions will encourage your child to try new songs and will give him a sense of accomplishment.

Feel like twirling? Don't be afraid to move around and shake a little. Your child will delight in dancing along with you and finding new ways to move to the music.

ZOOM

Music therapy is often used with children who have Autism Spectrum Disorder (ASD). ASD children typically have difficulty using and understanding language as well as difficulty relating to people and having social and peer relationships. Music therapy gives them the opportunity to express their emotions.

LOVING LIFE

Violin

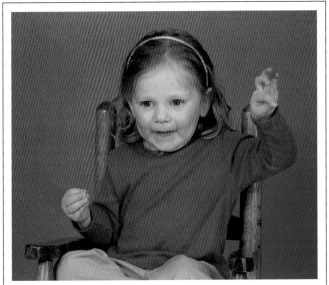

- *Violin* uses both hands. It is an iconic sign modeling one playing a violin.

- The stationary hand and arm pretend to hold a violin.

- Tilt the head as though it were resting on the chin pad of a violin.

- The dominant hand pretends to hold the bow and move it back and forth, playing the imaginary violin.

Horn

- *Horn* uses both hands.

- Like *violin*, this sign will look as though you are playing a type of horn.

- Use both hands to grasp an imaginary horn.

- Move the fingers as though you were playing the horn.

95

BIRTHDAYS

Celebrate growing older, bigger, and smarter with your toddler

A birthday party for a toddler can be an exciting event. At this age, the party can easily be kept simple, within a small budget and theme. Because it will involve little ones, it is a good idea to keep the party short—about an hour and a half is the limit for most young children. Within that period you will have enough time to eat cake and have a few activities. At age two, your child is still having primarily parallel play, rather than group play, so instead of inviting the whole neighborhood of similar aged kids, keep the party guest list confined to those most important to your child and your family.

Give your child two or three party theme ideas to choose from so he can have some control and can participate in the decision making. Perhaps a farm theme, a favorite character from television or a book, or even a favorite color—anything

Birthday Variations

- "Birthday" can be combined with other signs to create new concepts. Try these combinations using the sign for birthday and then:

- Birthday Party: Form the letter p with both hands and move from the wrist side to side.

- Birthday Cake: Place the stationary hand palm down and flat. Cup the dominant hand and place on top of the stationary hand. Move the hand up and down, on and off of the stationary hand several times.

Birthday

- ASL has many signs for *Birthday*. This popular version is easy for young children to sign.

- Begin with the middle finger of the dominant hand slightly bent forward.

- Place the middle finger on your chin.

- From the chin, move the middle finger to rest on your chest in the heart area.

- If you want to say *birthday boy* or *birthday girl*, add the sign for *boy* or *girl* after *birthday*.

can be the focal point of a toddler party. What is important is that your child gets to feel she is a part of the process.

Be sure to consider the time of day for the party when planning it. Nighttime may be more convenient for members of your family, but as you approach bedtime your child will become increasingly grumpy and less willing to celebrate. If your child still naps, you may want to make sure the party doesn't interfere with his schedule.

At this age, having a home party is easily achievable. Provide a variety of snacks that are age-appropriate and delicious.

You may opt to open the gifts from guests after everyone has gone home to minimize crying and hurt feelings.

The sign for balloon imitates blowing up a balloon.

Balloon: Part One

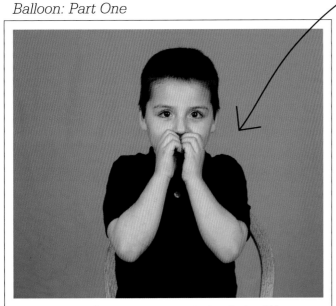

- *Balloon* uses both hands and the face.

- Begin by pretending to hold a balloon to your mouth with both hands.

- The hands should be in a loose O shape.

- Make an air bubble in your mouth to symbolize the blowing up of a balloon.

Balloon: Part Two

- Emulate the balloon inflating, with both hands opening up around an imaginary inflated balloon.

- The hands will no longer be in a loose O shape, but will now be slightly bent, with both palms facing one another.

PARTY TIME
Record and journal this special time of your child's life

Birthday parties are usually photographed and video-recorded. Taking the time to record important milestones in your child's life is a task worth doing. Preserving this special occasion through video and photo helps you remember your child just as he is today. You might even consider writing an annual birthday letter to your child to be ready one day when he is grown. You can include cute things your child said or did, what he liked or disliked, and anything exciting that happened throughout the year. By the time your child is 18 years old, you'll have a rich collection of memories to share with him.

By now your child should be signing a collection of words to you. Just as you record the first tooth, baby's first word, or first haircut, go ahead and make a journal about your signing

Candy

- *Candy* uses one hand only.

- Form the number 1 with the index finger of the dominant hand. All other fingers remain closed. (Refer to the number list in Chapter 19.)

- Place the finger on the side of the mouth. Use the same side as the hand you are signing with.

- Brush the finger downward two times.

Cake

The dominant hand will look as though it is writing a letter V over the stationary hand, much like a triangular slice of cake.

- *Cake* uses both hands. Begin with the stationary hand's palm facing up and flat. This hand will represent the cake being cut.

- Next, form the letter C with the dominant hand. Place the hand with the palm facing down toward the stationary hand.

- Move the dominant hand diagonally over the stationary hand. Then repeat the motion going the opposite direction. This motion represents cutting a piece of cake.

experience. If your child has invented some signs of his own, record which words and what prompted him to create the sign. Record when and what word is mastered and baby's response as he signs the word, and even consider taking a photograph by which to help remember the experience.

Taste

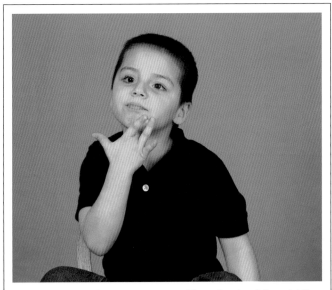

- *Taste* uses the dominant hand.

- Spread all five fingers apart. Slightly bend the middle finger forward.

- Place the tip of the middle finger near the lips. Next, move the finger back and forth to and away from the lips.

- Use your voice inflection here to reflect when something tastes good.

Good

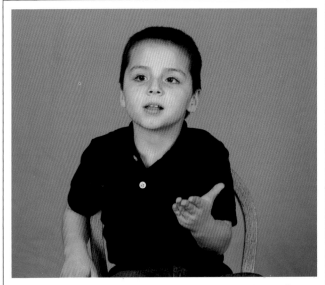

- *Good* uses both hands.

- The dominant hand begins by touching the chin. The palm faces your body and the fingers are straight and touching one another.

- Move the hand away from the chin until it rests in the flat stationary palm. The stationary palm is facing upward.

- Use an expression and tone that indicate that something is good.

FUN & CELEBRATIONS

MEETING NEW PEOPLE
Prepare your child for new experiences, people, and places

Meeting new people in strange settings can be an intimidating experience for a toddler. Many toddlers may become exceptionally clingy in new settings and around new faces. Don't worry if it seems your child wants to remain in your arms or attached to your leg while she gets comfortable. This is a normal reaction and allows her to feel secure despite an unfamiliar setting. Instead, consider this a bonding compliment.

You obviously have done a good job creating a safe and secure loving bond. Don't rush your child, but allow her to acclimate to the situation on her own time.

Before you introduce new faces, talk about where you are going and whom you will meet. If you know there will be another child, then talk about how your toddler can meet a new friend. Or, if there will be a pet, you can encourage

Name

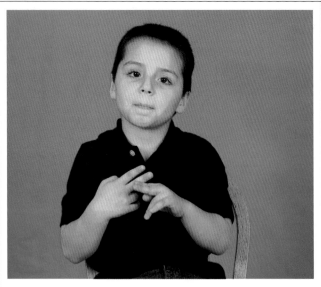

- *Name* uses both hands.

- Both hands form the letter H. Extend the index and middle fingers with all other fingers closed. (Refer to the American Manual Alphabet in Chapter 18.)

- Tap the dominant fingers on top of the stationary fingers two times.

- As you use this sign with your baby, repeat his or her name and reinforce that your name is Mommy or Daddy.

Hello

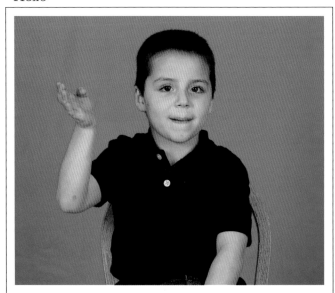

- *Hello* uses the dominant hand.

- Form the letter B. Fold the thumb across the palm with the remaining fingers straight and extended. (Refer to the American Manual Alphabet in Chapter 18.)

- Place the B on the side of the face. Use the same side as the hand you are signing with.

- Move the B upward and away from your face to say "Hello."

excitement by talking about the cute dog or cat they might see. Last, check your own emotions. Are you excited? Are you nervous? Or, are you calm? Your child will be aware of your emotions and tend to pick up and act on how you are feeling.

Here you will learn the signs *name*, *hello*, *good-bye*, and *friendly*. Before you meet a new person, have your toddler practice these signs. Use the sign *friendly* to talk about how to be friendly when meeting a stranger, or when discussing how a new person is friendly. After you sign *name,* try finger spelling your child's name. (Refer to the American Manual Alphabet in Chapter 18.) Though it is unlikely at this point that your child will be able to finger spell her name, you will be exposing her to hearing and seeing the letters of her name, which is great practice for preschool!

Good-bye

- Chances are your baby has already been signing *good-bye* to you.

- Simply wave or bend the hand back and forth to say "good-bye."

- Encourage baby to make this simple sign to everyone who leaves, or when baby is leaving a social event.

Friendly

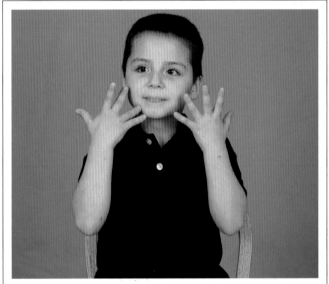

- *Friendly* uses both hands.

- Begin with both hands slightly in front of the face. Both palms will be facing your body.

- Have the fingers slightly spread apart. Wiggle the fingers as you move your hands backwards. The motion will end slightly behind your ears.

- Make sure your face looks happy and friendly and your tone sounds excited.

SPECIAL OUTINGS
Create a new and exciting memory with a simple and fun adventure

Special field trips with your child can either be a fun memory or a nightmare. Adventures require preparation to ensure they go just as you have planned. Pick a place where the toddler can have enough room to roam around and stretch. If the adventure confines the child to a stroller completely, you may be in for some tears. Take turns having a parent or family member be the point person in charge of the wandering toddler. If your special outing requires a drive, bring a grab bag of snacks and toys to help make the drive a little more entertaining.

Parks, playgrounds, and your own backyard are good, inexpensive, and toddler-friendly adventure sites. A farmers'

Party

- *Party* uses both hands. Begin by forming the letter P with each hand.

- The P is made by extending the middle and index finger with the thumb resting between them. The hand is facing downward. (Refer to the American Manual Alphabet in Chapter 18.)

- Simultaneously and in the same direction, move both hands back and forth.

- Repeat the motion several times.

Place

- *Place* uses both hands.

- Each hand forms a horizontal letter P using the index finger, middle finger and thumb. (Refer to the American Manual Alphabet in Chapter 18.)

- Place the hands so that the middle fingers are touching.

- Move the hands apart so that each hand creates a large horizontal half circle until the middle fingers touch and meet again completing the full circle.

market with free samples provides a variety of textures and smells to explore. Check out your local animal shelter or pet shop to visit animals.

Encourage grandparents to share an adventure with your child. The one-on-one time is a good way not only for them to connect and bond, but to give mom and dad a little alone time as well. If grandparents or other family members live far away, have a virtual adventure! Set up your Web cam and talk to grandparents or aunts and uncles.

········· • GREEN ● LIGHT • ·········

Raining outside? Have a picnic inside. Throw down an old blanket and set up a picnic in the middle of the living room floor. Use paper plates, sit cross-legged, and share a special rainy day meal. Not only will it break up the daily grind a bit, but it is a new adventure that can be done in your home and is completely free!

Prize or Award

- "Prize" uses both hands.

- Each hand will form the letter X. The X shape uses the index finger bent at both joints. The remaining fingers are closed. (Refer to the American Manual Alphabet in Chapter 18.)

- Position one hand in front of the other, one slightly higher than the other.

- Move both hands in an outward extension as though you were presenting a prize or award.

Picnic

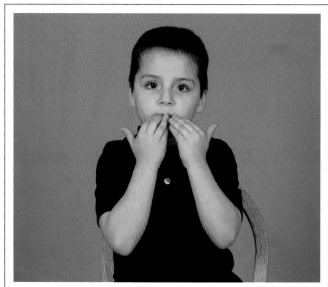

- *Picnic* uses both hands.

- Place both hands with the palms facing downward and fingertips at the lips.

- Bring both hands to the lips as though eating a sandwich or a meal.

FUN & CELEBRATIONS

103

BASIC INSTRUCTIONS
Basic instructions help you and your child communicate wants and desires

Here we will learn the signs *look*, *practice*, *come*, and **try**. These simple commands will help you and your child communicate more effectively with each other. One of the best advantages of sign language is the ability to use it despite the setting. If you are in a crowded room and you see that your child is distracted, the simple sign for *look* will communicate

instantly what you want your child to do. If you are interacting with multiple family members at once, perhaps reading a story or helping an older child with homework, you can simply sign a command across the room for the other child without causing interruption. In a library or bookstore quiet time, if your child begins to wander off, you can silently sign

Look

Communicate this sign with your facial expression as well as your hands.

- *Look* uses the dominant hand.

- Form the number 2 with the index and middle fingers of the dominant hand extended. (Refer to the number list in Chapter 19.)

- Place the fingertips pointing toward both eyes.

- Next, pull the hand away and turn the fingertips to face the direction in which you want the person to look.

Practice

- *Practice* uses both hands.

- Point the index finger of the stationary hand in a horizontal direction.

- Next, use the dominant hand to form the letter A with the fist closed and the

thumb pointing up. (Refer to the American Manual Alphabet in Chapter 18.)

- Move the letter A, fingers down, back and forth over the stationary finger several times.

and instruct your child to come to you.

These words are part of everyday conversation, so make sure you take advantage of using the signs every time you can. Sign language not only gives your child increased communication at an earlier age, increasing language and verbal development, but also provides a practical method of communication in any setting.

Come

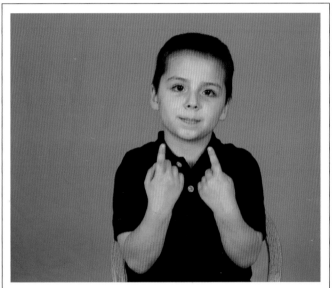

- *Come* uses both hands.

- Both hands are in the number 1 position with index fingers extended. Point the fingers outwards in front of you.

- Next, move the fingers simultaneously toward your body.

- This motion indicates that you want someone or something to come.

Try

- *Try* uses both hands.

- Form the letter T by placing the thumb between the index and middle finger in a fist position. (Refer to the American Manual Alphabet in Chapter 18.)

- Place both fists directly in front of you.

- Rotate from the wrists in an outward direction.

FEELINGS & EMOTIONS
Help your toddler understand and deal with his feelings and emotions

As your child continues to get older, she will begin to understand that her feelings have names. Helping your child label how she feels will give her a more complex understanding of good or mad or sad. Here you will learn the signs *scared*, *excited*, *shy*, and *surprise*.

At this age when feelings can still overwhelm their interac-

tions and communication abilities, some children revert to biting. If your child has taken to biting as an expression of his frustration or anger, begin to become proactive. Rather than yelling or punishing the child after the event, look for escalating moments when your child's frustrations are rising. In those sharing or playing moments, take a moment to step in and

Scared

- *Scared* uses both hands.

- Begin with both hands in a fist position on either side of your body.

- Move both fists toward the center of your body. As your hands near the center, change the fists into an open palm.

- The palms should be facing the body.

- Your expression and tone should look and sound scared and frightened.

Excited

- *Excited* uses both hands.

- Both hands make the same shape, with the fingers spread apart and the middle finger bent forward.

- Move the hands in alternating circles while both hands move forward.

diffuse the situation before a bite occurs. Let your child know that biting is not acceptable and that biting is not something your family does. Some children revert to biting as a means to gain more attention. Evaluate if perhaps your child is in a phase where he just needs more attention. Consider giving a little more one-on-one time to your child and see if it helps. Other children may bite as a result of being hungry. Monitor when the biting occurred in relation to the last meal or snack.

A biting toddler can be embarrassing and can enrage the parents of the child who was bitten. Be sure to be open about the situation, letting the parents of the victim know you are aware of what happened and are sorry for it, and how you intend to help resolve the biting.

Shy

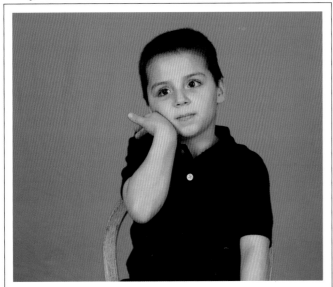

- *Shy* uses the dominant hand.

- Bend the hand and place the fingers against the side of the face. Use the same side of the face as the hand you are signing with.

- Slowly twist the hand forward as it rests against your cheek.

- Your voice and facial expression should also look shy.

Surprise

- *Surprise* uses both hands.

- Begin with both hands on either side of the face. The index finger and thumb are touching with the remaining fingers closed.

- As you say the word "Surprise," open the index finger and thumb apart.

- While the fingertips are moving apart, try to make your eyes wider as though you are thoroughly surprised.

107

WILD ANIMALS

Is a tiger or a fox one of your child's favorite things? Create a sign book of favorite things

Does your child especially love tigers? Or perhaps he is enamored of other wild animals, farm animals, or even favorite foods. Consider combining all of those favorites into a personalized sign book.

Creating a personal sign book for your child is easy and will help reinforce signs as well as provide another opportunity to use sign with your child. First, using a digital camera, photograph the important things in your child's life. Include parents, siblings, pets, grandparents, a favorite blanket or animal, pacifier, cup, favorite foods, and favorite toys. Next, print the pictures on your printer or have pictures printed from a photo shop. (You could also use cut out pictures from magazines or

Deer

- *Deer* uses both hands.

- The *deer* sign looks much like the antlers on a buck.

- Hold both hands with the palms facing outward, with the hand slightly bent and fingers spread apart.

- Place the thumbs on either side of the top of the head.

Fox

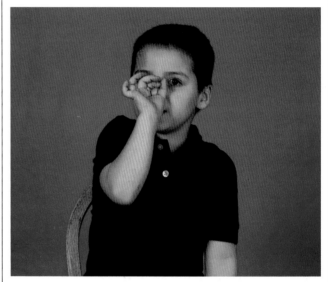

- *Fox* uses only one hand.

- Form the letter F, with the index finger touching the thumb to form a circle. The remaining three fingers are extended and spread apart. (Refer to the American Manual Alphabet in Chapter 18.)

- Place the circle of the F shape about an inch away from your nose.

- Twist the hand sideways twice.

old books.) If your child is able to recognize letters, then you might want to go ahead and label each item. Laminate the pictures to increase their life and durability.

Make the book as simple or as complex as you want it to be. If you are creative, you might consider making a fun cover and back page featuring pictures of your child with those favorite items. To bind the pictures together, you can either visit your local copy center, which has a variety of binding options, or you can bind the photos yourself using round binder clips, ribbon, or heavy-duty string or twine.

While looking at the book, pause at each photo allowing enough time for your child to sign. Take the book in the car or place it in the high chair or booster as you fix dinner. Show it to extended family and grandparents so they can learn your child's favorite signs too! As your child's favorite things begin to change, simply replace or add to the collection of pictures. You'll create a useful tool to reinforce sign language while creating a keepsake of your child's favorite things.

Tiger

- *Tiger* uses both hands.

- The hands are in a loose number 5 position with all fingers spread out and extended. The hands should be slightly bent, resembling claws.

- Begin with the hands on either side of the face.

- Move the hands back across the face.

Raccoon

- The *raccoon* sign uses both hands to emulate the mask on a raccoon's face.

- Form the number 2 with index and middle fingers extended. Place the finger-tips on either side of the eyes.

- Pull the hands away from the eyes, changing the shape of the fingers into the R shape for *raccoon*.

- *R* is made by crossing the index and middle fingers, much like you might cross your fingers for good luck. (Refer to the American Manual Alphabet in Chapter 18.)

FRIENDLY ANIMALS
Introduce others to your child's favorite signs

Going on a trip to the family farm or visiting a zoo? Learn the signs for the animals you will see ahead of time. That way you can begin introducing the signs as you talk about and build anticipation of the trip. Try to find pictures in books or online so your child will easily recognize the animals and be able to identify them with her signed words.

Seeing your child understand words through signing is exciting. You'll want to be sure that you're not the only one benefiting from your child's ability to talk with her hands. If your child has figured out that using her hands to communicate is successful, then likely you are not the only ones seeing her signs. As much as possible, try to teach and encourage those

Sheep: Part One

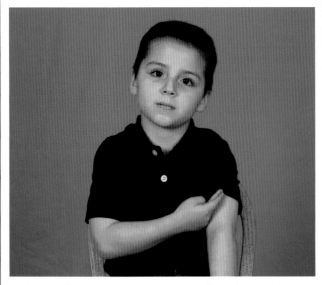

- The sign for *sheep* represents how a sheep's wool is cut.

- Begin with the stationary arm placed in front of your body. The fist is closed and facing downwards.

- Next form the number 2 with the index and middle fingers of the dominant hand extended. Turn the hand so that the palm is facing upward. (Refer to the number list in Chapter 19.)

Sheep: Part Two

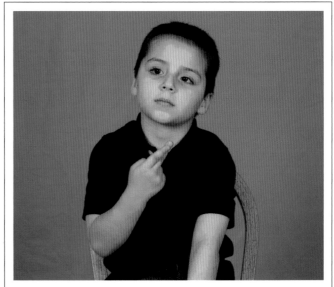

- Open and close the number 2 as though it is a pair of scissors trimming the wool.

- Move the dominant hand in the cutting motion up the length of the stationary arm.

- If you want to talk about a lamb, then first sign the word *small* before signing *sheep*.

- Try making the *baa baa* sound as you teach your child the sign for *sheep*.

in your child's life to use signs as well. At the minimum, grandparents, babysitters, and child-care providers can all easily be taught the most frequently used words. Having more people sign with your child will reinforce what is learned and will also make your child understood by more people. Increased communication for everyone is better!

Rabbit

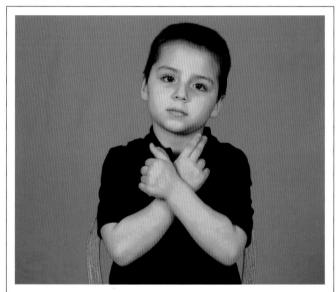

- *Rabbit* uses both hands.

- Cross the arms in an X-like formation.

- Extend the index and middle fingers, representing a rabbit's ears.

- Fold the fingers simultaneously back and forth several times, as though the ears of the rabbit are moving.

Kangaroo

- *Kangaroo* uses both hands.

- Bend both hands as though they are the legs of a kangaroo.

- Next, in a hopping motion move both hands simultaneously forward, imitating the hopping of a kangaroo.

ANIMALS AT HOME

Interacting with animals at home helps you evaluate how your two-year-old is doing

Here we will learn the signs *pet*, *bird*, *fish*, and *squirrel*. By two years old your child should be saying these words in combination with other words. As you watch your child interact with your house pets, other family members, and friends, try to take an objective look at how your child is progressing.

It's always a good idea to periodically check to see if your child is meeting or exceeding key developmental milestones. If you have concerns or questions it is a good idea to bring them to your doctor. While some issues may be no cause for worry, checking out any concerns ensures your child will continue to stay on track developmentally, reducing the need for intervention later.

Pet

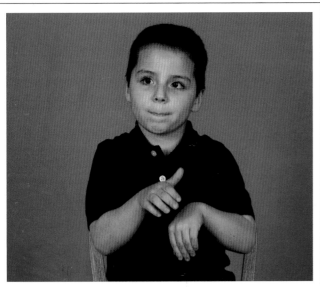

- The *pet* sign emulates the motion made when petting a cat or dog.

- The stationary hand is slightly cupped with the palm facing downward.

- The dominant hand lightly strokes the top of the stationary hand.

- As you teach your child *pet*, make sure the tone in your voice sounds gentle, as though you are giving the animal a gentle pat.

Bird

- *Bird* uses one hand only.

- Use the thumb and index finger of the dominant hand to form a "beak."

- Place the "beak" on the side of the face. Use the same side as the hand you are signing with.

- The thumb and the index finger close and open again, much like a bird's beak opening and closing.

2-year milestone check

Physical:

Walking and beginning to run.

Climbing on and off of furniture unassisted.

Able to pull something behind him while walking.

Able to kick a ball.

Able to stand on tip toes.

Able to color or scribble.

Begins to show signs of left- or right-handedness.

Builds towers with blocks or other objects.

Cognitive:

Forms two- to four-word sentences.

Forms simple phrases.

Recognizes body parts; be able to point to familiar objects.

Follows simple commands.

Demonstrates social independence.

Begins to exercise independence through defiance and saying "No."

Fish

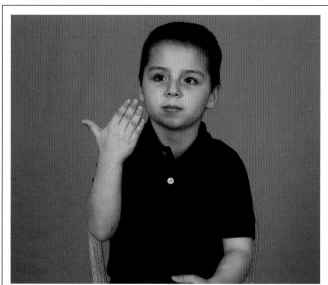

- *Fish* uses the dominant hand.

- The palm faces your body and the hand is slightly bent.

- Move the hand back and forth as you move the hand across. This motion will look like a fish swimming in water.

Chipmunk or Squirrel

- Form the number 2 with both hands, index and middle fingers extended. Face both hands together so thumb, pinky, and ring fingers of both hands are touching.

- Slightly bend the tips of the index and middle fingers. The fingertips of both hands will be opposite one another.

- Place hands about 2 inches away from your face so that fingers are about nose level.

- With wrists still touching, move hands inward and outward two times.

- This motion should resemble the whiskers of a chipmunk or squirrel.

COMPUTER TIME
A computer can be a great tool to enhance cognitive development in your toddler

When used appropriately, computers can be a great supplementary tool for cognitive development. When used alongside creative play, outdoor play, books, and other hands-on learning activities, computers can provide a great teaching resource. Software exists for teaching sign language, science, simple math concepts, ABCs, matching, pre-reading, and more to help grow and develop your toddler's young mind. Here we will learn the signs *computer*, *game*, *on*, and *off*.

When used in moderation, a computer can help strengthen and teach your child problem-solving skills, as well as improve hand-eye coordination. Follow up new computer knowledge with real-life application. For example, if you have just learned

Computer

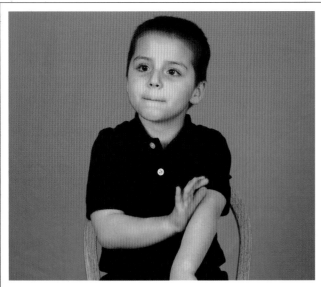

- Form the letter C with the dominant hand by curving all of the fingers and thumb. (Refer to the American Manual Alphabet in Chapter 18.)

- Place the C on the stationary arm slightly above the elbow.

- Brush the C up and repeat the motion.

Game

- *Game* uses both hands.

- Begin with the hands in letter A positions. The fists are closed and the thumbs are pointing upwards.

- Both fists begin about shoulder distance apart.

- Move the fists together until they meet. Bring the fists apart and together again.

about animals, go to a zoo and see the animal in person. Or, if you have just learned how to cook a simple recipe, practice it in the kitchen with your child.

It is best to wait until your child is at least two years old before using the computer to ensure that she has the necessary attention span as well as the coordination to move a mouse. Remember, the computer is best used when you are available to help your child learn and explore.

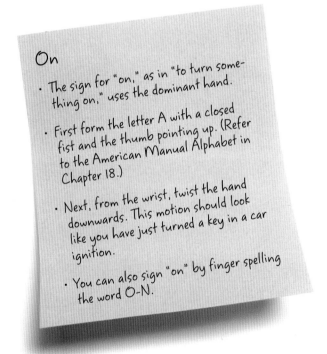

On
- The sign for "on," as in "to turn something on," uses the dominant hand.
- First form the letter A with a closed fist and the thumb pointing up. (Refer to the American Manual Alphabet in Chapter 18.)
- Next, from the wrist, twist the hand downwards. This motion should look like you have just turned a key in a car ignition.
- You can also sign "on" by finger spelling the word O-N.

Off

- *Off* is signed by finger spelling the word O-F-F quickly while moving the hand outward. (Refer to the American Manual Alphabet in Chapter 18.)

- *O* is signed by closing all fingers to touch the thumb.

- F is formed by closing the index finger and thumb together while leaving the other three fingers extended.

- To simplify this sign, consider just signing the letter F while saying "Off."

OUTSIDE & IN

AROUND THE HOUSE

Knowing where all the doors and windows are helps your family develop an effective fire safety plan

Teaching your child the signs for *door*, *room*, *window*, and *basement* has great practical value every day. You can easily instruct your child to open or close a door, or go to a room or basement, by just using your hands. Teaching your child awareness of these locations is also vital when an emergency strikes.

The Home Safety Council offers these recommended steps to prevent a catastrophe in your home:

Install smoke alarms on every level of your home, preferably alarms equipped with ionization and photoelectric sensors. Those alarms provide the best coverage.

Test the alarms each month. If your smoke alarms are over

Door

- *Door* uses both hands.

- Each hand will form the letter B, with the four fingers straight and extended, and the thumb folded across the center of the palm. (Refer to the American Manual Alphabet in Chapter 18.)

- Place the hands side by side, touching one another. The palms should be facing away from the body.

- Next, open the hands simultaneously toward your body. This should look like a door opening.

Room

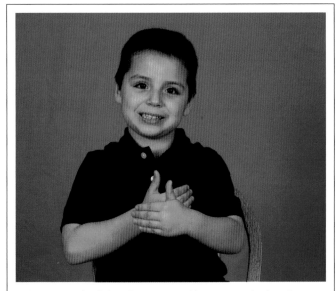

- *Room* uses both hands.

- The hands will be forming a box. Begin with both hands straight. Line the hands up to form the vertical lines of a box.

- Next, move the hands to form the horizontal lines of the box.

- The box is representative of a room.

10 years old, then it is time to replace them. Replace the batteries at minimum once per year.

Develop a fire escape plan of which the whole family is aware. Create a meeting place in front of your home in the event of a fire. Practice and run through the plan periodically.

Have a plan to wake up the younger children.

Check windows to be sure all of them can be opened.

Determine two ways to exit from each room.

Teach stop/drop/roll/and cool if one's clothes catch on fire. Cross both hands over the chest. Cool burned areas with water and seek medical attention for burns.

Exit the building or home first, then call for help using a neighbor's phone or a cell phone. Do not attempt to call 911 or emergency help while you are still inside.

Never go back inside a burning building or home for any reason.

For additional tools and resources on preventing fire in your home, visit the Home Safety Council Web site at www.home safetycouncil.org.

Window

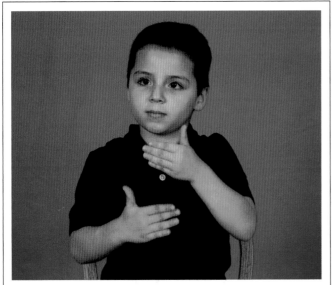

- *Window* uses both hands.

- Both palms face the body. Place the dominant hand on top of the stationary hand.

- Have the fingers closed together with no spaces between them.

- Move the dominant hand up and down as though it were a window opening and closing.

Basement

- *Basement* uses both hands.

- Hold the stationary hand flat, palm facing downward. This hand represents the ground level.

- Move the dominant hand in a circular motion underneath the stationary hand. This represents the basement area.

WHERE THINGS GO
Teach toddlers responsibility and have them contribute to household chores

Rather than picking up all the toys and putting them away yourself, or cleaning up spills unassisted, consider letting your toddler participate. Though it will undoubtedly take a little longer to accomplish your task, you will be teaching your child a life-long sense of responsibility and desire to help with chores. Additionally, as you do these activities with a good attitude and encouragement, your child will have a positive association and feel proud when she is able to accomplish responsibilities on her own.

Every day, have your child help you clean up the toys and help you put away any books. Sing a cleanup song as you clean to make it more fun.

Open

- Begin with both hands in the letter B position. All fingers will be extended with the thumb pressed in the center. (Refer to the American Manual Alphabet in Chapter 18.)

- Place both hands beside each other with the thumbs touching.

- Open the hands until they are both apart and the pinky fingers are facing the ground.

- The motion should mimic a door opening.

Close

- *Close* uses both hands.

- Begin with both hands in the letter B position. The four fingers are extended with the thumb across the palm.

- Both hands face outward, about shoulder width apart.

- Bring both hands together until they are touching. The index fingers and thumbs of both hands will be touching.

- This motion demonstrates the act of something closing.

If something spills, rather than becoming upset with your child, ask your child to get a towel to help clean it up. When you load the washing machine, have your child help you throw in a few pieces of clothing. As you empty and fold clothes, have your child help sort socks or group her clothes together in a pile separate from the big people clothes.

As you sweep the floor, let your child have her own broom and encourage her to help you sweep too!

Cabinet

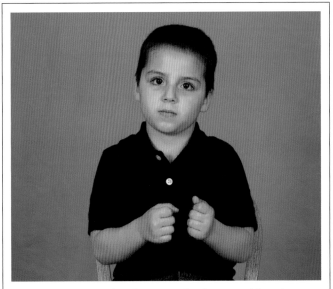

- *Cabinet* uses both hands.

- Place both hands in a closed fist at about chest level.

- The hands should look as though they are holding the knobs on a cabinet door.

- Simultaneously move both fists apart and away from one another as though they are opening a cabinet door.

Shelf

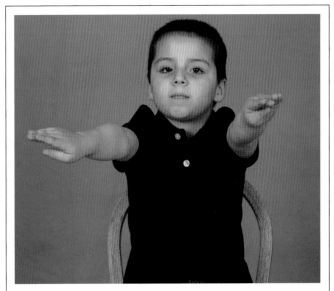

- *Shelf* uses both hands.

- Begin with both hands forming the letter B. The four fingers are extended with the thumb placed across the palm.

- Position the hands so that the palms are flat, facing down.

- Begin with both hands touching at the thumbs and index fingers.

- Draw the hands apart to represent a flat shelf.

119

OUTSIDE & IN

PRIMARY COLORS

Is that sign *blue* or *yellow*? Having sign confusion?
What to do if you don't understand

It isn't unusual for children who are learning many signs at once to begin to form their own signs, or use similar signs interchangeably for one another. For example, here you will learn two signs that have a similar motion—**blue** and **yellow**. What distinguishes these two signs is that one is formed with the letter B and one is formed with the letter Y. These letter cues make sense and are easy to remember as an adult, but for a toddler who is still learning letters, these subtle cues won't be very helpful. Instead, your child will associate the back and forth movement of the hand with both of these colors, and may pick the one that is easier for him to sign and use it for both colors.

Red

- *Red* uses the dominant hand. Form the letter R. Your index finger and middle finger will be crossed, similar to what you might do if you were crossing your fingers for good luck. (Refer to the American Manual Alphabet in Chapter 18.) Or, as an alternative, use just the index finger.

- Place the letter R or index finger to rest over your top lip, just below your nose.

- Brush the fingers away from the lip and onto it again. Repeat this motion twice.

Blue

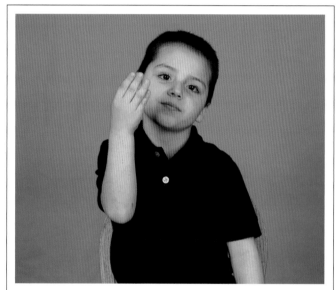

- *Blue* uses your dominant hand.

- Form your hand into the B shape. Your four fingers will be extended and close together. The thumb will be folded across the palm.

- From the wrist, move the hand back and forth several times.

You may discover that your child is trying to use a sign or gesture that you don't recognize. Or perhaps your child has created his own variation of a sign. Be mindful not to overcorrect your child. Instead of telling your child he is doing it wrong, try to figure out what sign your child is trying to say by examining the context. Then simply say and model the right way to sign. Chances are that over time your child will self-correct. If your child doesn't self-correct, that's okay too. Remember, you are trying to enhance communication with your child. If you understand what your child is trying to say, then you've achieved success! The fact that it may not be the perfect ASL sign is okay. Relax and don't be overly rigid on getting the sign perfect.

Yellow

- *Yellow* makes the same back-and-forth motion as *blue*.

- Begin with the letter Y. Your pinky finger and thumb will be extended out, while the middle three fingers are closed.

- From the wrist, move the hand back and forth several times.

Black

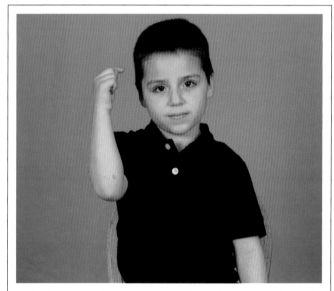

- *Black* uses the dominant hand.

- Form the number 1 with the index finger extended. (Refer to the number list in Chapter 19.)

- Place the finger horizontally in the center of the forehead over the same side eyebrow as the hand you are signing with.

- Draw the finger away from your head.

SECONDARY COLORS

Do I need to teach *green, orange, purple,* and *pink* if my child can say them? Why continue signing?

Until your child is able to be talk in full conversations, you will absolutely benefit from the continued use of sign language with your child. Incorporating sign language will continue to help language development. By understanding words conceptually, your child's verbal and language acquisition skills are being enhanced. If your child is beginning to communicate with a collection of words, signs still give your child a larger vocabulary for the words that are tough to say, or have not yet been learned.

Now that your child is a little older, you've probably noticed that he is learning and repeating the signs much more quickly than he was when he was only eight or nine months

Green

- *Green* uses the dominant hand.

- Form the letter G with the index finger and thumb extended. (Refer to the American Manual Alphabet in Chapter 18.)

- Move the G back and forth several times.

- Take advantage of the opportunity to ask your child to hear the *g* sound in *green*. Show him how you are forming the letter G as you sign.

Orange

The color orange and the fruit orange can be two different signs. Feel free to use just one to reduce confusion.

- Cup the dominant hand around the mouth and squeeze the hand together and apart again. This is symbolic of an orange being squeezed.

- Another version of *orange*, which is specific to the color

- orange, is to form the letter I with both hands with the pinky fingers extended, all other fingers closed. (Refer to the American Manual Alphabet in Chapter 18.)

- Swirl the pinky fingers around one another.

old. This increased ability to learn the signs helps your child rapidly increase his vocabulary when verbally speaking the words is still more difficult than using his hands.

Even once your child is conversing completely in verbal language, you'll find signs are often convenient in quiet places such as the library or church, or at the pool underwater, or even in loud places or when you are across the room from one another.

Purple

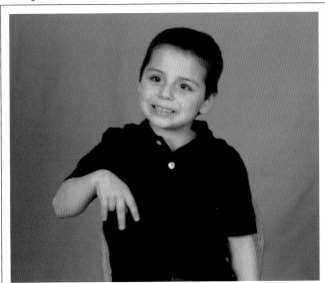

- *Purple* uses the dominant hand. Like the sign for *green*, *purple* begins with its first letter, P.

- Form P by placing the thumb between the index finger and middle finger. Point the fingertips downward.

- Shake the hand back and forth. Again, ask your child to hear the *p* sound and show her how the letter P is used in the sign.

Pink

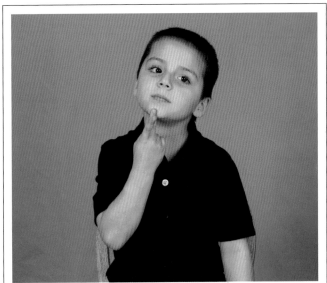

- *Pink* uses the dominant hand.

- Form the letter P and place the fingertips near the mouth.

- Move the hand up and down several times.

- Point out to your child how pink starts with P, and how the letter P is being used in this sign.

LIGHT & DARK
Take a moment to evaluate your progress before moving on

Signing should enhance your relationship with your child. As a result of consistent and regular signing, you and your child should understand one another better. If these signs are not increasing communication and understanding or if you are feeling frustrated, then it's time to stop and evaluate what you are doing.

Too many signs? If you are feeling frustrated, then chances are your child is picking up on that frustration and is feeling it too. Pick the signs that best work for you and your routine. Don't integrate signs you won't use often. Form some building block basics and build on those.

Communication hindered? Do you feel like instead of increased communication you are just finger fumbling? Then slow down. There is no need to try to integrate signs

KNACK BABY SIGN LANGUAGE

White

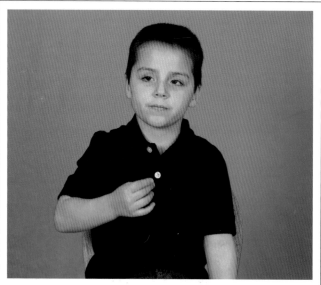

- *White* is formed using your dominant hand.

- Place the hand over the heart region of your chest. Fingertips will be touching your chest.

- Next, pull your hand away from your body. Draw the fingertips together as you say the word. The sign will end with all of the fingertips meeting.

- Take advantage of the many times to use this sign. Is the cat's fur white? The snow outside? Colors are everywhere, so take advantage of the opportunity to point them out and sign them.

Gray

- *Gray* uses both hands.

- Both hands will be facing the body with the fingers apart and fingertips slightly touching. Next, alternately move one hand through the other so the tips of the fingertips lightly brush as each hand takes a turn going to front and then to back again.

you have not yet mastered yourself. These signs should be helping you, not hurting you.

Not seeing success? How consistent are you with the signs? Remember, only consistent use of the signs in your routine throughout the day, every day is going to yield success. Part-time signing will not bring about success.

Light

Use your facial expression and tone to help convey the meaning of light and dark.

- *Light* uses both hands.

- Place both hands just below the chest with the middle fingers of each hand touching or slightly away the body.

- Next, lift and move away from the body both hands simultaneously. Continue to move the hands upwards until both hands are on either side of the face.

Dark

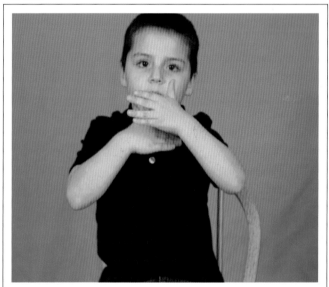

- *Dark* uses both hands.

- Begin with each hand in an open palm, facing your body.

- The movement will begin with the hands on either side of the face.

- Next, cross the hands in front of one another and in front of the face. Try to have a dark expression and use a low tone of voice to help convey the meaning of *dark*.

KEEPING HEALTHY
Does your toddler have doctor anxiety? Help alleviate anxiety and make doctor visits less stressful

It's not unusual for children to develop a fear of the doctor's office. Just remembering the last round of shots can be enough to send the most social child into a panic attack. If you are about to head into the doctor or dentist's office, then you might consider using signs as you talk about and prepare for the visit. Though it may seem wise to avoid mention-ing the doctor altogether, not talking about it won't help the anxiety levels once you are there. Talking about the doctor's office and describing how mommy and daddy also go to the doctor and dentist is a good place to start.

Once you have scheduled an appointment, pick up a toy or inexpensive stethoscope and role-play the visit. Pretend

Doctor

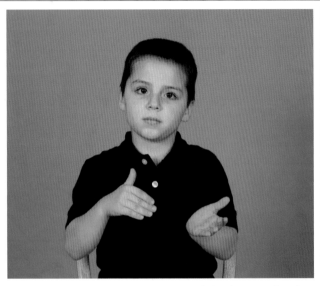

- *Doctor* is made using both hands.

- The stationary hand will be palm facing upwards and horizontal.

- Bend the dominant hand with the fingertips facing the stationary hand.

- Tap the fingertips on and off the open palm several times.

Dentist

- *Dentist* can be signed by placing the fingertips of the hand near the mouth. Move the hand toward the back of the head as though your mouth is being inspected.

- Or, form the letter D with your dominant hand. (Refer to the American Manual Alphabet in Chapter 18.)

- Knock the D back and forth close to the lips of your mouth to symbolize the dentist.

to look in the child's ears and listen to her heart, and then let your toddler take a turn. If your child will get a shot, let her give you a pretend shot and put a Band-Aid on you. Help her express her feelings through the role-playing activity.

Any time you head to the doctor, talk about what to expect. Have your toddler pick out a few special books or a coloring activity you two can do together while you wait in the office. Last, talk up the positives of the visit—perhaps your doctor has a prize drawer or a bowl of stickers or sugar-free lollipops. Whatever the prize is, make a big deal out of it and discuss what possible treasure your child may receive. You might even consider a post-doctor treat, like an ice cream cone or frozen yogurt, a new book, or a trip to the park.

Pain

- Form a number 1 with both hands. (Refer to the number list in Chapter 19.)

- Place the hands so the index fingers are facing one another.

- From the wrists, twist the hands in opposite directions.

Medicine

- *Medicine* uses both hands.

- Hold the stationary hand with the palm facing up, fingers together.

- The dominant middle finger touches the center of the stationary palm. Slightly move the finger back and forth.

EVERYDAY ERRANDS
Time for baby's first haircut? Help make the cut safe and fun for your toddler

With a little bit of planning the first haircut can be fun and set the tone for future cuts. Many areas now have salons that are designed for little people. Your child can get her hair cut while sitting inside a racecar or wearing a princess tiara. Many child-centered salons have movies or video games to help distract children. Because the focus is the children,

everything in these salons is child-friendly, including the hairdressers, the equipment, and the décor. Unlike going into a grown-up salon where your crying child may be embarrassing, in these salons you are safely in the company of other parents whose children have the same fears and anxieties or excitement as yours.

Barber or Haircut

- To say *barber* or *haircut*, you will use both hands.

- Form the letter V with both hands. (Refer to the American Manual Alphabet in Chapter 18.) The V represents scissors.

- Move the fingers together and apart again, resembling the cutting of scissors.

- Make this motion over your head as though you are cutting your hair. Begin at the front of your head, moving toward the back.

Library

- *Library* uses the dominant hand.

- Form the letter L using the thumb and index finger. This will look much like the written letter L.

- In the signing space in front of you, move the L in small circles. The palm is facing away from your body.

If possible, make an appointment and avoid a long wait as a walk-in. Waiting a long time can turn even the happiest child into a fussy toddler. You can schedule an appointment around your toddler's best time of day. Do not set the appointment too close to nap time, or too soon afterwards. Waking up your toddler early from a nap may make her cranky and uncooperative. Purposefully plan so your appointment can go as well as possible.

Mail or Letter

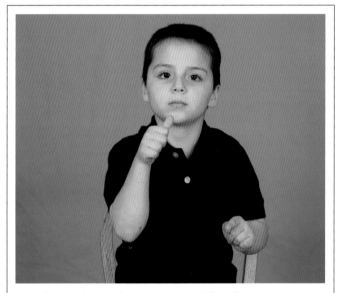

- *Mail* and *letter* are the same sign. You will use both hands for this sign.

- Begin by brushing the thumb against the mouth. This mimics licking a stamp.

- Holding the stationary hand with the palm facing up, place the thumb on the stationary palm. This will look like you are placing the stamp on the envelope (the stationary hand).

Bank

- In ASL, the sign for *bank* is made by finger spelling the word: B-A-N-K.

- The goal for your child is communication, and your child is probably not ready to begin spelling *bank* yet. Alternatively, just use the letter B.

- To form the letter B, extend all four fingers straight and pressed together. Press the thumb against the center of the palm.

- Take advantage of the opportunity to emphasize the *b* sound and encourage your child to think of other words with the letter *b* sound.

TRANSPORTATION
Make the most of your journey by talking as you commute

Traveling to your destination can often be as fun as the actual event. Here we will learn the signs *bus*, *taxi*, *subway*, and *motorcycle*. Use these signs as you see these modes of transportation in action or as you choose one to go on. While en route to your destination, open up the lines of communication. Talking about where you are going and what you will do helps build anticipation and encourages conversation.

In these beginning conversations you are likely to hear some adorable mispronunciations. The first time your child mispronounces a word you'll be tempted to chuckle. You may, however, be inadvertently encouraging your child not to speak. If your child feels as though you are laughing at him, he may be less likely to try new words or signs. Create a safe language environment by modeling the right way to say

Bus

- The ASL for *bus* can be signed by finger spelling the word: B-U-S. (Refer to the American Manual Alphabet in Chapter 18.)

- When your child is ready to begin learning simple three-letter words, then go ahead

and finger spell this sign.

- Until then, try using the letter B and extending the B outwards as though it were moving along the length of a bus.

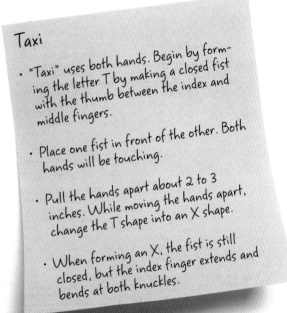

Taxi

- "Taxi" uses both hands. Begin by forming the letter T by making a closed fist with the thumb between the index and middle fingers.

- Place one fist in front of the other. Both hands will be touching.

- Pull the hands apart about 2 to 3 inches. While moving the hands apart, change the T shape into an X shape.

- When forming an X, the fist is still closed, but the index finger extends and bends at both knuckles.

words, without pointing out errors and correcting. Save the smiling and marveling at the cute expressions for when your child is not around.

When your child does begin to speak in sentences, resist the urge to interrupt. Let him finish his thought. Whether he speaks slowly or quickly, don't try to alter his tempo, but listen and let him speak, allowing his confidence to build. If your child chooses silence, don't try to force him to talk constantly. If your child states an opinion about something, don't be dismissive. Giving your child a safe place to talk and express words, signs, and emotions will help create a better bond between you and child and will also create a stronger, more confident verbal child.

Subway

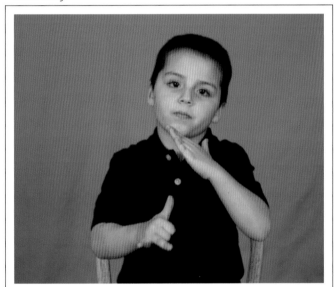

- *Subway* uses both hands.

- Hold the stationary hand with the palm facing downwards and flat. This represents the ground level.

- The dominant hand forms the letter Y. The pinky and thumb will be extended with the three middle fingers closed. (Refer to the American Manual Alphabet in Chapter 18.)

- Move the Y underneath the stationary hand, side to side. This represents the subway underground.

Motorcycle

- *Motorcycle* uses both hands.

- Each hand pretends to grasp the handlebars of the motorcycle.

- Move the hands back and forth as though they are holding the handles and accelerating.

- Have fun with this sign by making the *vroom vroom* sound of a motorcycle.

PLAY BASEBALL
Outdoor activities such as baseball help thwart childhood obesity

Being active doesn't have to cost a fortune. Pick up an inexpensive plastic toddler-sized bat and ball and have some old-fashioned baseball fun with your child. Getting outside and letting your child swing at the tee or catch a few balls is a great way to help encourage a life of activity and healthy choices.

Sadly, childhood obesity is an ever-growing epidemic in North America. While your child is young you have the most impact and opportunity to shape your toddler's eating habits, setting the stage for healthy eating habits later. Don't wait to get started.

Begin at the grocery store. Your child isn't the one who is making the food selections and purchases. What comes through your door is your choice. Just as you monitor what

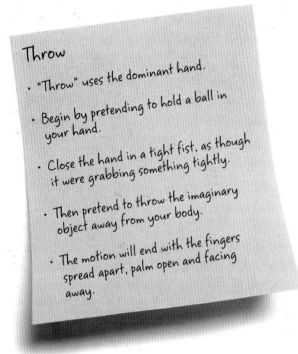

Throw

- "Throw" uses the dominant hand.

- Begin by pretending to hold a ball in your hand.

- Close the hand in a tight fist, as though it were grabbing something tightly.

- Then pretend to throw the imaginary object away from your body.

- The motion will end with the fingers spread apart, palm open and facing away.

Walk

- *Walk* uses both hands.

- Each palm will be facing downward.

- Move one hand in front of the other as though it were one foot walking in front of the other.

- Make the motion several times to give the illusion of someone taking steps.

your child watches and sees, you are also the gatekeeper of your child's health. If you don't want your child to snack on unhealthy foods, don't bring them into the home.

Throw the clean-plate syndrome out the window. Instead, look to make sure your child is eating balanced portions of healthful choices. Are you encouraging overeating by providing too much food? When your child stops eating or appears to be full, don't push it by forcing your child to continue eating.

Be balanced. While healthy food choices should always be the goal, it is okay to indulge in a cookie or a special treat at times. Try not to reward with food if possible, but be wary of too much deprivation.

Stay active. Healthy eating is just one part of the equation. How much physical activity you and your child get is equally important. Go outside when weather allows. You don't need a gym to be active. Model activity by not turning on the tube all the time, and show your child a life of living, not sitting.

Swing

- *Swing* uses both hands. Grip both hands around an imaginary bat.

- Act as though you were swinging at the ball with the bat.

- *Swing*, the noun, as in a swing on the playground, is not made the same way.

- Instead, it is made using the *sit* sign with the dominant fingers bent, as though it were a chair or swing. Move both hands back and forth in a rocking motion.

Slide

- *Slide* uses both hands.

- Hold the stationary hand flat, palm facing upward.

- The dominant hand forms a bent number 2, palm facing upwards. (Refer to the number list in Chapter 19.)

- Place the 2 on the stationary hand at the bottom of the palm.

- In a sliding motion move the 2 across the palm of the hand until it reaches the fingertips.

FEED THE ANIMALS
A day at the petting zoo is a great way to interact with animals face to face

A petting zoo is a terrific opportunity to give your child first-hand exposure to animals that she might not normally see. Here, she can safely pet a goat, feed some geese, and touch some fur. It is also a great time to put your signing skills to use. Encourage her to sign and talk about the animals before you head to the zoo, while you are there, and as you drive

home. To help your petting zoo visit remain a fun experience, take a few cautionary measures.

First, if you are with small children, supervise and monitor them at all times. If you are going with a group of parents or class, don't use this time to catch up. Keep your eyes focused on the children. Though the zoo is meant for children, little

Feed

- *Feed* uses both hands.

- Fold both hands so that the thumb and fingertips are touching.

- One hand will be higher than the other. Move both hands outwards as though you are feeding something or someone.

- Bring the hands forward and down two times, emulating this feeding motion.

Animal or Animals

- *Animal* uses both hands.

- Place each hand just below each shoulder. Place the fingertips on the chest. The fingers remain straight.

- From the wrist, move the hands toward each other twice.

tools, wire, and even the food for the animals can pose potential hazards.

Second, talk about how this is not the time for a pacifier, thumb-sucking, eating food, or for putting the hands in the mouth at all. *E. coli* bacteria are the greatest threats at these petting zoos. This is not the time for the five-second rule. If a pacifier is dropped, put it away.

Third, come prepared. Though most petting zoos have areas for washing hands or antibacterial gel dispensers, bring your own wipes and gel to be safe. Use them frequently and liberally, especially after petting animals.

Last, use warm soapy water to wash the hands when you leave to ensure prevention against *E. coli* bacteria contamination. *E. coli* bacteria can cause diarrhea and vomiting, and can even require hospitalization.

Goose

- Using your dominant hand, close the thumb, index finger, and middle finger together.

- Place the fingers by the mouth as though the fingers are the bill of a goose.

- Open and close the thumb from the index finger and middle finger as though the bill is opening and closing.

Goat

- *Goat* uses the dominant hand.

- Form the ASL number 3 using the thumb, index finger, and middle finger. Close the ring and pinky fingers. (Refer to the number list in Chapter 19.)

- First, open the 3 on the forehead. Next, move the hand to the chin and open the 3 on the chin.

- This motion resembles the horns on the head and the furry beard on the chin.

VISIT A PARK
Teach your toddler how to be a good steward of the environment

The environment and the rise of global atmospheric temperatures are a concern to everybody. You don't have to be a staunch activist to make little changes that can have a global impact. Just as parents should model good stewardship for money, talents, and time, we should also model good stewardship of our planet. A trip to the park is a great time to talk about the earth and being responsible.

Take a trash bag to the park and pick up cans or paper. Avoid picking up dangerous items such as broken glass or cigarette butts by asking your child to choose a specific item to collect. Next, deposit the collected items in your recycling bin. Not only will you teach your child about recycling, but you will also teach her to care about her community and to give back to it through something as easy as picking up a bit of trash.

Tree

- *Tree* uses both hands and arms.

- The stationary hand and arm will lie horizontal, facing the ground. The palm is flat.

- The dominant hand is in a number 5 position. (Refer to the number list in Chapter 19.)

- Place the dominant elbow on top of the stationary palm. Rotate the hand back and forth twice.

Grass

- *Grass* uses the dominant hand.

- Form a loose number 5, with fingers slightly bent.

- Place the hand, palm facing down, underneath your chin.

- Make a circular motion with the hand. When the back of the hand is near the chin, lightly brush it against the bottom of the chin. Repeat the circular motion two times.

Instead of bringing prepackaged water bottles to the park, instead fill your own water jugs or water bottles. Not only will you save a few cents by bringing your own, you'll avoid creating trash that will either fill landfills or have to be recycled.

Encourage safe and respectful play at the park. If your child wants to take home various rocks or other artifacts, discuss how it is a good idea to leave nature as she found it. Explain how important it is to leave those little treasures for others to discover and learn from as well.

Once back at home look for ways to expand the life of products. Give away or sell outgrown clothes, pieces of furniture, or other items that still have usability and life left. If you repurpose a piece of furniture around the house, talk about how doing something so simple helped save a tree. Integrate little lessons of environmental stewardship throughout your day.

Wind or Windy

- *Wind* uses both hands.

- Form both hands in a loose number 5 position. The palms of each hand face one another.

- Simultaneously move both hands one direction, with one hand slightly higher than the other.

- Next, move both hands simultaneously in the opposite direction. This motion should look like wind blowing back and forth.

- Feel free to make a blowing sound as you make this sign.

Clouds or Cloudy

- *Clouds* will use both hands.

- Form the letter C with both hands facing one another. (Refer to the American Manual Alphabet in Chapter 18.)

- While looking up, with hands about face level, simultaneously move both hands inward, toward your body from your wrist. This should look like one cloud.

- Repeat the motion in the center area now. Next, repeat the motion again on the side opposite where you started. So you will make the sign three times in a row in front of your face.

HELP IN THE GARDEN
Ready to get dirty? Dig your way to a garden good time

Next time you are ready to plant some flowers and spend some time in the yard, let your toddler get involved. It might take just a bit longer to get your gardening done, but you and your toddler can use this opportunity to be physical, to talk with your hands, and to learn about gardening together. Here we will learn the signs *dig*, *plant*, *seed*, and *flower*.

Child-sized gardening gloves, boots, watering pails, and tools are available inexpensively at most large retailers. Giving your child her own set of gloves and tools will foster excitement and prepare her for a day outdoors.

Give her a small pot or area in the garden that she can have exclusively. For the younger ones, simply letting them dig and water can be enough to entertain them for hours. As your child gets older, let her plant a few seeds and have her own

Dig

- Pretend to grasp both hands around a shovel.

- Move both hands simultaneously downwards as though you are digging into the ground.

- Next, scoop both hands up as if the pretend shovel has just finished digging a hole.

Plant

- *Plant* can use one or both hands.

- Pretend to grasp seeds in your hand or hands.

- Rub the fingers of the hand together as though you are sprinkling seeds into the ground or pot.

- This is the sign for the verb, *to plant*. To sign the noun *plant*, simply sign the word for *grow* two times in a row.

garden. Use the opportunity to talk about proper watering, sunlight, and food for the plants. If you've just planted flowers or shrubs that need a good watering, turn on the hose and let your toddler help. She'll delight in making patterns with the spray. If it is warm enough outside, put on her swimsuit and don't worry about getting wet. Delighting in dirt and water is wholesome fun that is cheap and entertaining.

In colder weather, give a child a bag and encourage her to collect acorns. Or, rake up a pile of leaves to jump in or bury each other. Yard work can be fun and productive.

Remember, every time you are outside with your small child constant supervision is required. Tools, hoses, buckets of water, small stones, acorns and passersby can all be potential threats.

Seed

- *Seed* uses both hands.

- Extend the index finger of the stationary hand outwards in a horizontal number 1 position.

- Next, form the letter X with the index finger of the dominant hand. The index finger will be bent at both joints while all other fingers are closed. (Refer to the American Manual Alphabet in Chapter 18.)

- Dot the fingertip of the X on the stationary index finger three times in a row along the finger. This action should emulate three seeds being planted.

Flower

- *Flower* uses the dominant hand. Begin by closing the thumb to the other four fingers.

- Place the hand on one side of the nose.

- Next, move the hand to the other side of the nose.

- You can begin on either the left or right side.

SEASONAL ACTIVITIES

Whatever the season, make sure your toddler is covered in sun protection

Teaching seasonal signs may seem like a lot of work for such a short window of time, but you can use these signs all throughout the year. When you talk about sledding, you reinforce other winter signs like *snow*, how it is close to favorite winter holidays, and family traditions or celebrations. On blustery winter days, have a digital slide show of summer fun and refresh your child's memory of warm weather activities such as swimming, 4th of July, fireworks, and more. Seasonal signs can help set a foundation for understanding seasons and learning the months of the year. Here we will learn the signs for *sled, umbrella, kick* and *splash.*

No matter the season, avoiding overexposure to the sun is

Sled

- *Sled* uses both hands.

- Place one hand on top of the other hand, both palms facing up.

- Move the hands away from the body at a downward angle, representing a sled moving down a hill.

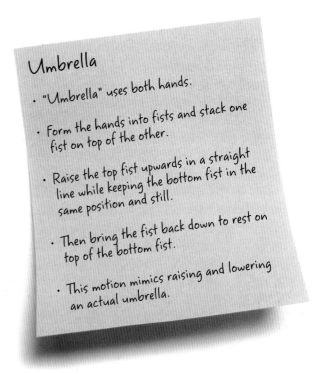

Umbrella

- "Umbrella" uses both hands.

- Form the hands into fists and stack one fist on top of the other.

- Raise the top fist upwards in a straight line while keeping the bottom fist in the same position and still.

- Then bring the fist back down to rest on top of the bottom fist.

- This motion mimics raising and lowering an actual umbrella.

important. Any sunburn, especially those that blister, raises the risk of developing serious forms of skin cancer. So, it is important that every time your child is outside she is covered and protected.

The first line of defense for your child is clothing. In cooler weather, make sure your child's arms and legs are covered and keep a hat on his head. In warmer temperatures, look for shade if possible.

Because UV rays are emitted even on cloudy days, covering your child in an SPF 15 sunscreen is always a good idea.

MAKE IT EASY

Create a flash card sign game to help hone your child's signing skills. Or, use a felt board to display the pictures. Photograph your child's favorite objects, activities, family members, pet, foods, and more. Print off the photos. To extend the life of the photos, laminate them. If using a felt board, apply a piece of Velcro on the back of each photo. Go through the pictures and sign the words as you say them.

Kick

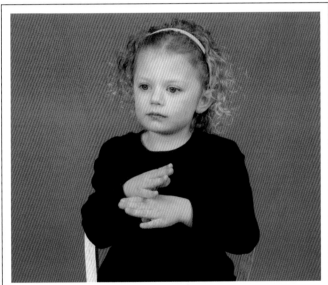

- *Kick* uses both hands. The dominant hand will strike the stationary hand, showing the action of kicking something.

- Both hands have flat palms, fingers together.

- Hold both hands sideways, thumbs facing upward. Move the dominant hand underneath the stationary hand until it strikes the bottom of the hand.

Splash

- "Splash" uses both hands.

- Begin with both hands in a closed fist, palms facing away from the body. Cross both fists forming a big x.

- Uncross both fists while opening the hands. Both hands will open wide, fingers spread apart.

- Be expressive! The face should look shocked as though someone has just splashed water on you by surprise!

141

PRETEND TO COOK

Cooking in the kitchen is fun for everyone. Inspire creativity with food

The first signs you introduced to your child probably centered around mealtime and eating food. Now it's time to think about involving her in the excitement of cooking. As you mix, spread, sprinkle, and taste, take the extra moment to sign these simple words—*cook*, *pot*, *mix*, and *bowl*—with your toddler.

Are you doubtful that your toddler can handle cooking quite yet? Though the time for complex recipes or using the stove or oven has not yet come, that doesn't mean she can't have fun cooking. Here are some ideas to get you started:

Give her a small bowl of Nutella, jam, or any other delicious spread. Provide graham crackers, Saltines, or club crackers.

Cook

- *Cook* uses both hands.

- Hold the stationary hand with the palm facing upwards.

- Place the dominant palm on top of the stationary palm. Next, flip the domi-

nant hand over so that the palm is now facing upward.

- This motion looks much like a pancake or hamburger being flipped.

Pot

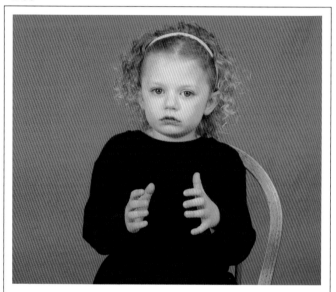

- *Pot* is formed much like *bowl*, but the sign will be larger.

- *Pot* uses both hands. Begin with both palms facing upward. The hands will be touching at the pinky fingers.

- Bring the hands apart and upward, forming a large bowl-like shape.

Let your child practice spreading on the cracker. It's okay if it is messy. Letting her practice will make her feel big and will expose her to new textures. If you want to take it to the next step, provide a few toppings to sprinkle on top—raisins, nuts, coconut, chopped fruit; use your imagination.

Make your own pizza. Use a pre-baked pizza crust or a refrigerated pizza crust, or make your own. Let your toddler help spread the tomato sauce, sprinkle the mozzarella cheese, and add any other toppings he would like to include. He will feel proud to have helped cook dinner!

Give your child a tortilla or wrap, or a leaf of lettuce. Provide slices of lunch meat and cheese. Let her lay the ingredients on the wrap and roll up the sandwich.

After you've created a culinary masterpiece, encourage your toddler to help clean up afterward. Help her put back boxes and other items she can carry. Or, give her a towel to wipe off a countertop and have her help you rinse out a bowl.

Mix

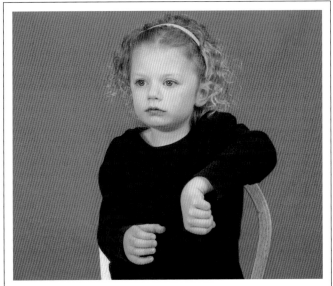

- *Mix* uses both hands.

- Form the number 5 with both hands. Bend the fingers slightly.

- One hand will be facing the other hand. Simultaneously and in alternate directions move the hands in a circular motion.

- This sign is symbolic of things being mixed around together.

Bowl

- *Bowl* uses both hands.

- This motion is similar to *pot*, but is much smaller in size, resembling a bowl.

- Begin with both pinky fingers touching, palms facing upward.

- Draw apart the hands into a bowl-like shape. Keep the motion small, in proportion to a bowl.

143

A DAY OUT
Keep a day at the park or playground safe and fun

Going to the playground is a fun event for any toddler. Though they are still too young to understand who strangers are just yet, there are things you can do proactively to keep your child safe from predators.

As cute as those monogrammed backpacks, blankets, and T-shirts are, avoid putting your child's name directly on her. This is an easy way for a predator to learn the name of your child. If a predator calls your child by name, it is more likely that your child will feel at ease and will let his guard down. Older children who are called by name will be less likely to think this potential predator is a stranger because the person knows his name. Instead of monograms, find other distinctive ways to identify your child's belongings. Assign each child an animal or object, such as a train or dinosaur, and use

Let's Go

- *Let's go* uses one hand.

- Slightly cup the hand and place it in the center of the chest.

- Pull the hand outwards while simultaneously closing the hand.

- The movement should look like something moving out.

Movie

- *Movie* uses both hands.

- The stationary hand will be straight, palm flat and vertical. There should be no spaces between the fingers.

- The dominant hand will be straight and flat, with fingers together. Place the dominant hand horizontally on the stationary hand.

- Move the dominant hand up and down two times.

that to personalize the things that belong to him.

It goes without saying that if you are taking your child to a playground, to the movies, or to another special activity, you must plan on supervising your child. As much as you can, avoid cell phone use and talking with passersby to avoid inadvertently looking away. Despite your best intentions it only takes a second for a child to dart away. Talk with your child about the danger of traffic and cars and how streets and parking lots are off-limits without a grown-up. Hopefully, if your child does suddenly decide to explore a new area,

knowing that streets and parking lots are off-limits will keep him in a safer area.

Before you go anywhere, always remind your child what to do if he or she suddenly can't find mommy or daddy. Encourage him to seek out a uniformed person or another mommy for help.

Playground: Part One

- *Playground* is a compound sign made up of two words: *play* and *ground*. Here we will learn the first word, *play*.

- Form the letter Y with both hands. The pinky finger and the thumb will be extended while the middle three fingers are closed. (Refer

  to the American Manual Alphabet in Chapter 18.)

- From the wrist, move both hands back and forth two times, toward your body and then away from your body.

Playground: Part Two

This is the sign for "ground."

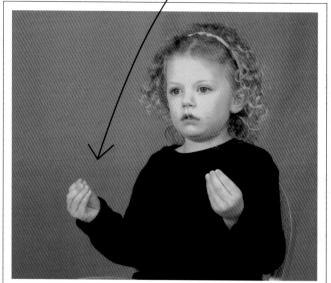

- To complete *playground* you will need to sign *ground*.

- *Ground* uses both hands.

- Close both hands together so that the fingertips are touching the thumb. The palms will be facing upwards.

- Move the thumbs around in circles as though feeling dirt between the fingers.

145

TIME PASSES

Teaching basic time concepts helps toddlers and preschoolers understand the order of the day

Your young child probably knows more about time than you might think. For example, he knows that when he wakes up it is morning and that he eats breakfast. He knows that lunch comes after a morning of play. He knows that dinner comes after naptime and playtime. He knows that bedtime comes at the end of the day, and if you have a bedtime routine, he can predict what is coming next and just how close bedtime is. Here we will learn the signs *watch* or *time*, *maybe*, *before*, and *after*. These are great signs to use when talking about when things happen in relation to one another.

To help encourage your child to be even more aware of time, work with her on numbers 1 to 12. Count out Cheerios,

Watch or Time

Your child should easily learn this sign, since this is probably what you do naturally when discussing time.

- *Watch* or *time* uses both hands.

- The stationary arm and hand will be extended slightly in front of you. Close your palm into a fist. Keep the palm face-down.

- The dominant hand will form the number 1. Tap the index finger of the number 1 on top of the wrist where a watch would be.

- Tap the wrist several times.

Maybe

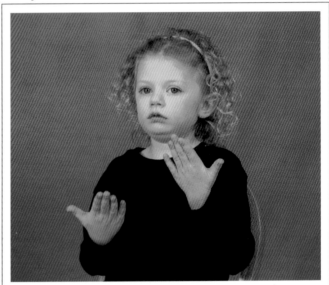

- *Maybe* uses both hands.

- Both hands will be flat, palms facing upward. Place one hand higher than the other.

- Simultaneously move the top hand down while moving the bottom hand up. Repeat this motion several times.

- Be sure to have a questioning expression.

crackers, pennies, or other small objects. Once she can identify these numbers, point them out in everyday interactions. Help her discover where the numbers are on the clock. Knowing what these numbers look like will help her figure out the time on a digital clock, and later help her read an analog clock. When your child becomes a little older she will have a great foundation for telling time.

· · · · · · · · · GREEN ● LIGHT · · · · · · · · ·

Have you started singing the ABCs to your child yet? Putting the alphabet to song makes learning and memorizing the ABCs easier. Your child may not be able to say every letter, but the song will be yet another tool to help her learn. If you want to take the ABCs to the next level, use the ASL alphabet in Chapter 18. These letters are used in many of the ASL signs.

Before

- *Before* uses the dominant hand.

- Place the dominant hand in a number 5 position with the palm up. (Refer to the number list in Chapter 19.)

- Begin the sign with the palm slightly lowered, almost flat.

- Move the hand upward until it is straight up and down, completely facing your body.

After

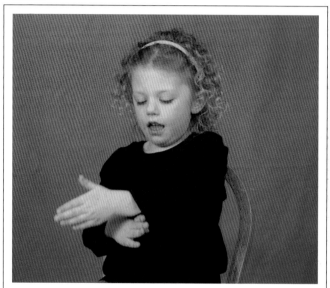

- *After* uses both hands.

- Place the stationary hand palm facing the ground.

- Move the dominant hand over the stationary hand.

- The dominant hand will be sideways, with the pinky finger facing the ground.

- Move the dominant hand away from your body.

FARM SCENE

Add more farm signs for story time, playtime, or an actual visit to the farm

Farms are a favorite topic of picture books and imaginary play toys for children. When your child plays on the ground with her toy farm animals or barn, take a moment to get on the floor and play too, using signs and talking about the animals as you play. As you read aloud to your child, incorporate all your farm animals and farm scene signs. Here we will learn the signs *barn*, *tractor,* and *grow*.

Are you reading every day? Reading out loud to your child not only creates a special bond between parent and child, but it provides a wealth of knowledge about language. Though your child may hear words in everyday conversation, reading provides a specific time when your child will

Barn

- *Barn* uses both hands.

- Place both hands together so that the fingertips of the hands are touching.

- The tips of the hands should look like they are forming a roof.

- Next, move the hands in a straight downward motion as though they are the walls of the barn.

Tractor

- *Tractor* uses both hands.

- Imagine that you are holding the wheel of a large tractor.

- Place both hands on an imaginary very large wheel and pretend to drive, moving the hands slightly back and forth.

- The size of the imaginary wheel helps distinguish this sign from *car* and *drive*.

148

learn about the sequence of a story, hear inflection in your voice, and understand concepts. As you or she asks questions about the story, she is learning important social skills as well. Coupling the use of signs while you read only enriches the reading experience.

Signing the complete "Grow" sign twice is also the sign for the noun "plant."

Grow: Part One

- *Grow* uses both hands.

- The stationary hand will form a horizontal letter C. (Refer to the American Manual Alphabet in Chapter 18.)

- Cup the dominant hand

together so the fingertips of the dominant hand are touching the thumb.

- Place the dominant hand with fingertips pointing up just under the stationary hand.

Grow: Part Two

- Now that the dominant hand is just under the stationary hand, begin to push the dominant hand through the horizontal C.

- As the hand emerges through the C, it remains closed with fingertips touching the thumb.

- As the wrist and hand begin to push through, extend the fingers open. This should look like a flower that has just emerged from a planted seed.

149

ON THE WATER
Learn signs for on and off the water

Headed for some wet and wild fun? These signs—**boat**, **fishing**, **swim**, and **breathe**—are great for water. Because breathing is taught in swim lessons, *breathe* is a great sign to learn here. When your little one becomes a proficient swimmer, take your signs underwater and have an underwater conversation. While on the lake, signs are great to use when the loud engine can make it hard to hear what is being said. Your

child will be able to tell you when she's hungry, when she wants to swim or fish, or if she needs a bathroom break, no matter how loud it is on the water.

All boats are required to have one life jacket per occupant on board. Everyone should wear one. Children under age 13 should never be on the water without a life jacket.

Life jackets are also helpful if you are headed to a commu-

Boat

- *Boat* uses two hands.

- Slightly cup each palm. Place the hands together with the pinky fingers touching.

- Move the hands up and down simultaneously as though the hands were a boat going over rough waves.

Fishing

- *Fishing* uses both hands.

- Grip the stationary hand around an imaginary reel.

- Use the dominant hand to grasp an imaginary pole.

- Slightly move the arms simultaneously back and forth to mimic having a fish on the line.

nity pool where it is difficult to keep your eyes on your child at all times. Every year, more than 1,300 children under age 14 die needlessly from drowning. Supervision is essential to prevent these deaths. Even in pools or beaches where lifeguards are present, drowning can still occur. Be safe.

Swim

- *Swim* is an iconic sign using both hands.

- Place each hand palm down in a letter B position, with the four fingers straight and the thumb resting across the palm.

- Begin with both hands together. Index fingers and thumbs of each hand will be touching.

- Bring the hands apart and together again as though you are swimming underwater.

Breathe

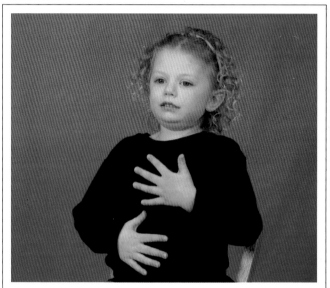

- *Breathe* uses both hands.

- Spread both hands apart and place them on your chest.

- Move the hands away from and back to your chest several times.

- The sign mimics the motion of a chest breathing up and down.

EXPLORATION & PLAY

VEHICLES

Help your child explore a real-life fire truck! Visiting a fire station is fun and educational

Here we will learn large moving-vehicle signs: *fire truck*, *airplane*, *helicopter*, and *rocket*. You may have toy versions of all these objects, or your child may enjoy reading about them in books, or even seeing them in action. Exposure to fire trucks and airplanes is not only exciting, it also teaches children not to be afraid of them. Seeing a fire truck on a road and actually

seeing a fireman can be two totally different experiences for a child.

A fire station tour is great because, first and foremost, your child will get to see what a fireman looks like with full gear on. If your child is unprepared, a fully dressed fireman can be scary. Knowing ahead of time what the clothes and protective

Fire Truck

- *Fire truck* in ASL is a compound sign. First make the sign for *fireman*.

- Sign *fireman* by placing the hand, palm facing out, on the top of the head like a large fireman's helmet.

- Next, make the sign for *drive* by pretending to drive a steering wheel.

Airplane

- *Airplane* is a one-handed sign.

- With the palm facing downward, extend the thumb, index and pinky fingers. The middle and ring finger are folded down.

- Move the hand outward as though it were a plane flying in the sky.

headgear look like will help reduce anxiety in an emergency situation. Second, your child will get to see, touch, and feel a fire truck, hoses, and ladders and see where firemen eat and sleep. Last, your child (and you) can learn fire safety tips. Because these tips are coming from a fire fighter firsthand, your child will probably tend to listen more than he would to mom or dad.

In today's security climate, your child's first experience with an airplane will probably be when you travel on one for the first time. Be sure to arrive early so you and your family can pre-board. Talk to the flight attendant about having your child look around, or perhaps even meet the captain before the flight. Let your child know what to expect during the flight, and be sure to bring backup snacks and entertainment.

Helicopter

- *Helicopter* uses both hands.

- Form the number 1 with the stationary hand. (Refer to the number list in Chapter 19.)

- Place the dominant palm face down on the index finger.

- Shake the dominant palm back and forth several times. This should resemble the propeller on top of the helicopter.

Rocket

- *Rocket* uses both hands.

- Hold the stationary hand horizontal, palm facing the ground.

- Cross the index and middle fingers of the dominant hand. Rest the base of the dominant palm on the back of the stationary hand.

- Next, move the crossed fingers upward and slightly side to side as though the rocket has just taken off into outer space.

JUST IMAGINE
Stage a play, create a castle, or make a time machine, all with just a cardboard box

Creative play allows your child to grow, learn, and play all while having fun and using his imagination. Through a costume or a puppet your child can suddenly become a superhero, an animal, a magician, or anyone he wants to be. A large box from a television or refrigerator, or just an old cardboard box in the garage, can instantly be transformed into a

time machine, rocket ship, fort, stage for puppets, or refuge for action figures. Don't be afraid to let your child make a little mess while having some great creative fun.

Pull out some washable markers, paints, or crayons and let your child decorate the box any way he wants.

Use glue and buttons, beads, old fabric, popsicle sticks,

Dress Up

- Begin with both hands in an open number 5 with all fingers spread and extended and palms down. (Refer to the number list in Chapter 19.)

- Place the thumb of each hand at the top of your chest.

- Simultaneously, brush thumbs outwards several times.

Play or Performance

- This sign means *play*, as in the theater, rather than the verb *to play*.

- Form the letter A with both hands using the thumb pressed on the side of a closed fist. (Refer to the American Manual Alphabet in Chapter 18.)

- Begin the sign with one hand forward away from the chest, and the other hand closer to the chest.

- Making large circles, simultaneously move the hands alternately toward the chest.

glitter, and uncooked noodles or beans to give your child another way to decorate his creation. Though your child is no longer a baby, it is still important to keep a watchful eye to avoid potential choking hazards.

Pull out old sheets and allow your child to add on to his fort by draping the sheet over the box or extending the fort to another box. If you have more than one box, your child can create a tunnel between boxes using the sheet as a covering.

Give your child a few days or so to take full advantage of the box. Sure, it might not be the most attractive addition to your family room, but the creative play and enjoyment your child will have are worth a few days of inconvenience. When you start to notice that the child's interest is waning, it might be time to get rid of the box.

Here we will learn the signs *dress up*, *play*, and *box*. Get creative, use your signs as you play, and have fun!

Box: Part One

- *Box* uses two hands.

- Begin with both hands flat and straight. The hands will be on their sides with the pinky fingers facing the ground.

- Begin with both hands pointing straight ahead. The palms will be facing one another.

- In this position the hands should resemble two sides of one box.

Box: Part Two

- After forming the first part of *box*, you'll demonstrate the other two sides of the box.

- Move the hands so that one hand is in front of the other. Both hands will remain sideways.

- Both hands will be facing the body.

155

LET'S HAVE LUNCH

Lunch doesn't have to be PB&J; new twists on lunch can make eating more fun

Peanut butter and jelly, while a good standby, isn't always the most palatable option. An enjoyable mealtime, from the food to the conversation whether verbal or signed, helps make lunch more than just another part of the day to get through.

As you consider these new lunch options, think about the signs you have already learned or signs you are about to learn

and how to incorporate them into mealtime:

Graham crackers and peanut butter. Peanut butter doesn't always have to go on bread. Let your child practice making a snack while he spreads the peanut butter on the cracker.

Cookie cutters aren't just for cookies. Are you helping your child study letters, shapes, or numbers? Or perhaps it is

Meat

The thumb and index finger should look like they are gripping a piece of meat.

- *Meat* uses both hands.

- The stationary hand is horizontal, in a number 5 position. The pinky finger faces the ground.

- Place the dominant thumb and index finger between the thumb and index finger

of the stationary hand. The dominant fingers grip the stationary hand.

- The middle, ring, and pinky fingers of the dominant hand are extended. Slightly move the dominant hand back and forth while keeping the stationary hand still.

Peach

- *Peach* uses one hand.

- Slightly cup the dominant hand and place it on the cheek.

- Place the hand on the same side as the signing hand.

- Move the hand in small circles about two or three times.

holiday time and you're looking for a little fun. Use cookie cutters on your sandwich to create fun shapes while reinforcing learning at the same time.

Want something warm, but you're in a rush? Pick up a rotisserie chicken from your local grocer or warehouse store. The chickens are usually well within the budget, provide many meals, and taste great eaten alone or in sandwiches, quesadillas, chicken salad, and more.

Wrap it up! Tortillas or sandwich wraps are available in a variety of flavors. Experiment with meat, cream cheese, jams, and more to create your own sandwiches. Your child will love helping make the creation and wrapping it up. Cut the sandwich into slices to make easy-to-hold spirals.

Break out some dips. A variety of low fat, tasty dip options such as hummus or yogurt makes fruit and veggies more fun to eat.

Sandwich

- *Sandwich* uses both hands.

- Place both hands near the mouth as though they were a sandwich.

- Next bring the hands into an open mouth as though you are about to take a bite of the sandwich.

- This is an easy sign for your child to use.

Vegetable

- *Vegetable* uses the dominant hand.

- Form the letter V, or number 2. The thumb, ring, and pinky finger are closed. (Refer to the American Manual Alphabet in Chapter 18.)

- Place the tip of the V on the side of the chin. Use the same side of the face as the signing hand.

- Pivot and twist the V back and forth on the tip of the index finger.

SNACK BREAK

Snack time is a part of every healthy diet, but how many snacks does your child really need?

There's a difference between healthy snacking and all-day grazing. Healthy snacking occurs at a designated time of day. It involves snacks that are nutritious and that provide enough sustenance to help your child make it to the next meal. Allowing your child to snack all day long can be detrimental to establishing healthy eating habits. Instead of your child learning cues for when he is hungry, he learns just to eat all day long. When snacking all day, it is unlikely that your child is making good choices about what he is putting in his mouth.

Snacks, like meals, should be served at the table. Don't allow your child to eat his snack in front of the television, and avoid

KNACK BABY SIGN LANGUAGE

Thirsty: Part A

- *Thirsty* uses the dominant hand.

- Place the index finger at the top of the throat.

- Some people sign thirsty using both the index finger and the thumb, in a letter G shape. Your child will probably find it easier to use the index finger.

Thirsty: Part B

- Move the finger down the length of your throat, symbolizing a thirsty throat. Your finger will end at the base of your throat.

- As you sign and speak *thirsty*, use inflection in voice and intensity in sign to reflect how thirsty you feel.

- Your child can use this sign quickly and easily to communicate to you that he is thirsty across the playground, in a quiet story time setting, and more.

feeding him a snack on the run. Establishing the routine of eating at the table helps encourage eating food at mealtime. If the child is allowed to eat on the run or throughout the day, he isn't going to be as likely to eat the meal that is set before him.

By the time your child is a preschooler, having three set meals and two snack times a day will provide plenty of eating opportunities while ensuring you aren't giving too much food.

Sweet

- Form the dominant hand in a number 5 position with the palm open and all fingers extended.

- Place the fingertips of the hand on the chin. The palm will be facing you.

- Brush and fold the fingertips off the chin.

- Repeat this motion.

Ice Cream

- *Ice cream* is an easy-to-learn sign that your child will quickly pick up.

- *Ice cream* uses the dominant hand gripped around an imaginary ice cream cone.

- Move the hand back and forth near the mouth as though you are eating the ice cream. Don't worry about pretending to lick it; the back and forth motion of the wrist emulating a cone says enough.

- Make the movement twice, as though you have just licked the cone twice.

GROWING UP

BRUSHING TEETH
Teach your preschooler good dental hygiene

The desire for good dental hygiene doesn't seem to come innately for most preschoolers. Playing with their toys, making a craft, having a snack, chasing the dog, or looking at a book is usually more entertaining than going to the bathroom to brush teeth. Getting into a routine and being consistent is the best way to teach your child that good dental hygiene is not an option.

Begin by leading and showing your child how to brush his

teeth. Let your child brush his own when he is ready. It is always a good idea to do a mouth check to ensure a proper brushing was done. Pick two times a day that you can make brushing teeth a habit, perhaps after breakfast and right before bed. Don't pick a high-stress time when you are trying to get out the door. Avoid giving "free passes" on teeth brushing because it sends the message that brushing is optional and doesn't

Stepstool

- Stepstool in ASL is a two-part sign. Since this application is to communicate with your child, you can choose to use both parts or just one part. Remember, the goal is communication, so use what helps you communicate best.

- The first part of *stepstool* is to form the sign for box.

- Next, use your dominant hand in an upside-down number 2 position. Move the fingertips to resemble someone standing on the box.

Toothbrush

- *Toothbrush* or *brush teeth* uses the dominant hand.

- Use your index finger to represent the toothbrush.

- Move it back and forth near the mouth to signify brushing teeth.

- If you want to say *toothpaste*, next make the motion of squeezing toothpaste from a tube into your hand after signing *toothbrush*.

160

have to be done every time. Your child should see a dentist about every six months for a cleaning and exam.

Have flossing and toothpaste options. Floss picks make flossing a little easier for children. Let them choose the color or design and give them some part of the decision. The same is true for toothpaste. Let your child pick the flavor or theme of the toothpaste. She may not be able to control whether brushing is an option, but at least she can decide which toothbrush, toothpaste, and floss go into her mouth.

Towel

- *Towel* uses both hands and arms. Each hand will look as though it is gripping a towel.

- Fists are on either side of the face, as though the towel is behind your neck.

- Move the fists simultaneously back and forth in the same direction. You should look as though the towel is drying off your neck.

Mirror

- *Mirror* uses the dominant hand.

- Cup the dominant hand in a slightly bent palm.

- Place the hand several inches away from the top of the head. Use the same side of head as the hand you are signing with.

- Move the hand back and forth from the wrist as though you are adjusting a mirror to look into.

GROWING UP

161

TOILET TIME
Tired of trying to tame the toilet? Use signs to make toilet time go more smoothly

Here we will learn the signs *flush*, *toilet*, *wipe*, and **underpants**. Using these signs with your younger child will help give him a way to communicate when he is able and ready to use the restroom, even if he is not able to verbally say so. If your child is older and is now beyond daytime training but is instead using an older child's nighttime disposable underwear, use

the diaper sign for the nighttime disposable pants. Throughout the day, ask your child with just a quick motion of the hand if he needs to use the restroom. Your child can answer discreetly and in any setting. Once in the restroom, teach your child good bathroom habits by reminding him to flush.

Making the transition to dry days and dry nights can be a

Flush

- *Flush* uses the dominant hand.

- Pretend to grasp a toilet flush lever with the dominant hand.

- Move it downward as though you are flushing.

- Have fun with this sign by adding the sound of the toilet flushing.

Toilet

- *Toilet* uses the dominant hand.

- Form the letter T with the dominant hand. The thumb will be tucked between the index and middle fingers.

- (Refer to the American Manual Alphabet in Chapter 18.)

- Shake the hand side-to-side.

bit stressful. To help encourage a stress-free nighttime routine, always make sure your child has used the restroom before going to bed. Though a wet bed means more work for mom and dad, scolding won't help your child make progress. Instead praise the successes and encourage him with stickers, certificates, or other forms of validation. By the time your child is five, dry nights should be the norm. If your child has experienced a stressful event, such as a death in the family or the birth of a new sibling, it could trigger an unusual bout of nighttime wetting. Try to talk to your child about his worries, and before long his bedtime habits should return to normal. If you have any concerns, you should speak to your pediatrician.

Wipe

- "Wipe" uses both hands.

- Begin with the palm of the stationary hand facing up.

- Make a closed fist with the dominant hand.

- Place the fist on the open palm. Move the fist around in a circular motion as though you are wiping the surface clean.

Underpants

- The sign for *underpants* uses both hands.

- Slightly extend the middle finger of each hand and place on the hips.

- Pull the fingers upwards as though you are pulling the pants up.

SETTLING DOWN
Winding down helps mom, dad, and child communicate better with one another

After a hectic day it is always a good idea to pause and reflect on the day. Here we will learn the signs *talk*, *feel*, *listen*, and *attention*—all signs you can use as you are trying to hear what your child is saying to you. You can also use these signs as you direct your child to listen in a reflective time or in a busy setting such as a store, park, or restaurant.

These signs can be tools to help you be more present with your child. Sharing the same space doesn't mean you are connecting emotionally. Take advantage of the cues these signs will give you. Encourage your child to talk to you about his day, and how it made him feel. Listen by responding and answering questions. Is your time with your child quality

Talk

- *Talk* uses both hands.

- Open both hands, palms facing outwards in a slightly cupped position. Place both hands at about chest level.

- Simultaneously, slightly move both hands backwards and forwards several times.

Feel

- *Feel* uses the dominant hand.

- Place the middle fingertip in the middle of the chest.

- Extend the other fingers.

- Move the fingertip outwards away from the chest and then place the fingertip back on the chest. Repeat the motion.

time? While quantity of time is certainly important for any child, if the time isn't quality as well, then it is just passing time for both of you.

The little mundane moments are when life happens. All of the tower-building, princess tea parties, car races, and pirate-playing are building relationship and connection between you and your child. These mundane moments will quickly pass. Enjoy the moments you have now. Tomorrow will come quickly enough. For today, be present. Enjoy the sidewalk, the stories, what your child smells like fresh out of the tub, the way she whispers "goodnight" to you, or delights when you come through the door. Enjoy the doing. The laundry, the dishes, the phone calls, the bills will always be with you, but your little one won't.

Listen

- *Listen* is made using the dominant hand.

- Either using the pointer finger or cupping the dominant hand, bring the hand toward your ear.

- Look as though you are trying to hear something.

- Speak the word "Listen" as you sign it.

Attention

- *Attention* uses both hands.

- Bring both hands to either side of the face. The hands will be flat, with no space between the fingers.

- Move the hands forward and back on either side of the face.

- Make sure your tone and facial expression are commanding attention.

STORY TIME

Reading aloud with your emerging reader helps instill important pre-reading skills

Reading aloud with your child will help establish the emerging reading skills your child needs to have literacy success. As you sit with your child reading, be sure to point out how reading occurs from left to right. If your child is able to identify letters, occasionally point one out and ask her what it is. Build her confidence with praise. Next, ask what sound the

letter makes. If she doesn't know, that's okay; take the opportunity to model the right sound.

Reading stories, repeating nursery rhymes, and singing finger play songs help children recognize important phonetic patterns. When a child understands that words are assembled blocks of sounds, they will have the phonetic awareness

Story: Part One

- *Story* uses both hands.

- Begin the sign with both hands apart, fingers slightly separated.

- Bring both hands together. Interlock the middle and thumb fingers together, forming a ring.

- After the hands have interlocked, pull them apart again.

Story: Part Two

- Next, change the direction of both hands. If the dominant hand was facing the body it will now face outward. If the stationary hand was facing outward it now will face the body.

- Once again bring both hands to interlock and pull them apart again.

- Last, turn the hands back to the original position and repeat the motion. In total your hands will interlock and come apart three times.

to begin forming and reading words. As you see letter combinations, point them out and help your child recognize those combinations in text. Help your child write and recognize her name with fun crafts, paints, and more.

Use your child's screen time to her advantage. When she does turn on the computer, give her games that reinforce the emerging reading skills she is developing. To get the most out of the computer time, sit with her and watch and guide if needed. Resist the urge to let the computer be the babysitter. Follow up with workbooks or fun activity pages while you wait in doctors' offices, at restaurants, or in a carpool waiting for an older sibling.

Here we will learn the signs *story*, *sit cross-legged*, and *lie down*. Use these signs during your individual or group story time. Remember to use other signs as you read aloud.

Sit Cross-Legged

- Sitting with the legs folded and crossed is important for circle or story time. This sign uses both hands.

- Each hand forms the letter X. X is formed by bending the index finger at both joints. All other fingers are closed. (Refer to the American Manual Alphabet in Chapter 18.)

- Rest one finger on top of the other finger.

Lie Down

- *Lie down* uses both hands.

- Place the stationary hand and arm flat and horizontal in front of your body.

- Next form the number 2 with the dominant hand. Hover the dominant hand just above the stationary hand and arm.

- Turn the 2 over so that the palm is now facing upwards and place it on top of the stationary hand and arm. This should resemble someone lying down on something.

CELEBRATIONS
Celebrating and remembering life can happen all year long

Ever notice that the older your child becomes, the less often the video camera comes out? Other than special holidays or birthdays many times that little device that was supposed to record your life often goes unused. Instead of being able to reflect on a collection of memories, you end up with holiday highlights. Using sign language with your child is a great reason to break out the camera. The preciousness of

communication in this moment is a memory you'll want to keep. Here are some other ideas to help inspire you to record the moment:

Several times a year, set up a tripod camera to record your family dinner time. Purposefully choose a night that's not a special occasion or a big meal. Over the years you'll have a special memory of how your family table dynamics looked

Celebrate

- *Celebrate* uses both hands at shoulder level.

- Both hands form the letter A with fists closed and thumbs pointing up. (Refer to the American Manual Alphabet in Chapter 18.)

- In a circular motion from the wrist, move each A in several circles simultaneously.

- Your expression should be excited and celebratory.

Holiday

- *Holiday* uses both hands.

- Form a loose number 5 with both hands. (Refer to the number list in Chapter 19.)

- Place the thumbs on the upper chest, just under the shoulders. Move the thumbs forward and away from the body and back two times.

and changed, and smile at the familiar meals served.

Photograph and record normal events. Heading out the door for a visit to Grandma's or a day at the beach? Don't just take a picture of what it looks like once you get there, but of the hustle and bustle along the way.

Record the down-on-the-floor moments. When dad or mom is playing monster, airplane, or just wrestle mania on the floor, take a moment to snap a quick picture or recording. It's moments like this that are the high point of your child's day, not the latest toy.

Every New Year's Eve (or other designated day) ask your children questions and record the answers. Ask what their favorite food is, what they want to be when they grow up, their favorite song, what they like to do with mom and dad. Over the years you'll develop a rich history of your child's thoughts.

Gift or Present

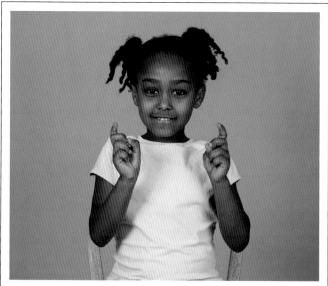

- *Gift* or *present* uses both hands.

- Create a loose letter X with both hands by bending each index finger at both joints.

- Curve the thumb toward the index finger. Keep all other fingers closed.

- Place one hand slightly in front of the other. Begin with the index finger almost upright. Then outwardly move the hand while rotating the index finger downward.

- This motion should look like you are presenting something to someone.

Family

- *Family* uses both hands.

- Begin with both hands forming the letter F with the index finger and thumb touching. The rest of the fingers are extended.

- Both hands touch at the index finger and thumb.

- The palms of each hand will be facing one another.

- Next, move each hand in a half circle until the pinky fingers of both hands meet. Both hands will be forming a circle together.

SPRING HOLIDAYS
Do holidays or large crowds spark shyness in your child?
Use signs and common sense to break the ice

Walking into a crowded room filled with guests can be intimidating for adults, and much more so for a child. If your holidays take you to crowds, consider how you can help ease your child's sudden onset of shyness:

Talk about where you are going before you get there. If a cousin, favorite aunt or uncle, or friend is going to be there, be sure to let him know so he has someone specific to look forward to seeing.

Even if your child isn't a chatterbox with strangers, encourage him to have good manners. Simply saying "Hi," and "Please" and "Thank you," will give your child a little more experience in a new and scary social setting.

St. Patrick's Day

- The *St. Patrick's Day* sign is based on the tradition of pinching a person who is not dressed in green.

- The motion imitates a pinch.

- The stationary arm is straight.

- Using the dominant hand, pretend to twist and pinch the arm near the shoulder.

Passover

- *Passover* uses both hands and arms.

- Bend the stationary arm. The forearm will be straight and close to the body.

- Tap the dominant fist or palm on the elbow of the stationary arm.

Bring along a favorite game or activity. If your child is unsure about joining the crowd, the game or activity can help ease him into the environment.

Check in on your child using the signs she has learned. You don't have to walk over and interrupt what your child is doing. Instead, use your signs to talk to your child regardless of the crowd or noise level. When your child catches your eye, simply sign to him and he can let you know if he is doing all right, is hungry, needs to use the restroom, is sleepy, or wants to go home.

Last, model good social skills. Be approachable, care about what people have to say, listen thoughtfully, and use good manners. When a child watches his parent be a good social role model, he is learning how to be one someday too.

Here are the signs for some fun family holidays when you can practice both signs and social skills: *St. Patrick's Day*, *Passover*, *Easter*, and *Easter bunny*.

Easter

- *Easter* uses the dominant hand.

- Form the letter E with the four fingertips folded on top of the thumb.

- Move the E from one side to the next in a slight arc motion. The E should look like it is tracing the handle of an Easter basket.

Easter Bunny

- Form both hands into the ASL number 3, which uses the thumbs, index, and middle fingers extended. (Refer to the number list in Chapter 19.)

- Place both hands on either side of the forehead.

- Move the index finger and middle finger back and forth like rabbit ears.

SUMMER HOLIDAYS

Though your child can now effectively verbalize summer fun, signing still has value

Summer days are filled with long hours at the pool or beach, fireworks, and good outdoor fun. Take advantage of summer fun opportunities to learn and integrate new signs into your vocabulary. Here we will learn the signs for *parade*, *barbecue*, *fireworks*, and *Fourth of July*.

By age three your child is communicating primarily through his words. At this age it may seem like the value of using sign language with your child is diminishing. Though using sign language is no longer needed for effective communication, signing with your preschooler still has great value. For example, if you choose to teach the American Manual Alphabet along with the ABCs, you are integrating another sense, which

Parade

- *Parade* uses both hands.

- Loosely form the number 5 with both hands. (Refer to the number list in Chapter 19.) Place one hand directly in front of the other with the fingertips facing downward.

- Simultaneously move both hands slightly up and down while moving both hands forward.

- The motion should look like a procession moving forward.

Barbecue

- *Barbecue* is made using the dominant hand.

- Finger spell the letters B-B-Q in order. Beginning with the letter B, extend four fingers up, closed together. The thumb rests against the palm. Repeat.

- Next, form the letter Q. Point the index finger and thumb toward the ground. The remaining fingers are closed.

increases memory retention and effective recall ability.

Signs also help give emerging readers a better conceptual understanding of words, which increases comprehension. Using signs encourages creative use of your preschooler's body. She can not only use her body for playing, running, sports, and dancing, but for talking as well. Last, in any situation where silence is needed or warranted, you can effectively communicate important messages such as *stop, listen,* and more with just one sign. The value of using sign extends well past the baby stage.

Fireworks

The motion for fireworks should look like fireworks exploding in the sky.

- The sign for *fireworks* uses both hands.

- Begin both hands with the fingertips and thumb touching.

- Alternate between quickly opening each hand, extending the index finger as though a firework has just exploded.

- Repeat this motion several times.

Fourth of July

- To say *Fourth of July*, you will first sign July, then the number 4. (Refer to the number list in Chapter 19.)

- *July* uses both hands. Begin with the stationary hand straight, with the thumb facing your body.

- Make the letter J with the dominant hand. (Refer to the American Manual Alphabet in Chapter 18.) Sweep the J along outside of the stationary hand.

- Next, form the letter Y. Sweep the thumb of the Y downward along the palm of the stationary hand.

HOLIDAYS

173

AUTUMN HOLIDAYS

Trips, visiting family, long meals . . . What are your family traditions?

When the autumn leaves begin to fall, we know that Thanksgiving and the holidays are just around the corner. This time is typically filled with family traditions and big meals. While your family is young, have you begun to think about what kind of traditions you wish to impart? Traditions provide rich memories for your child to grow up with and help frame expectations for holidays. What is important is that your traditions reflect what is of value and important to your family unit.

Traditions don't have to be what everyone else does. Far from family? You don't have to load up the kids for a cross-country journey. Create a new tradition in your own home. Invite neighbors or friends, or even reach out to immigrants in your community who are new to American holidays and

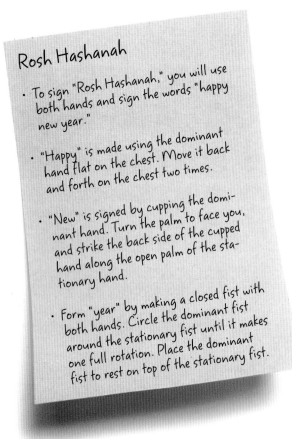

Rosh Hashanah

- To sign "Rosh Hashanah," you will use both hands and sign the words "happy new year."

- "Happy" is made using the dominant hand flat on the chest. Move it back and forth on the chest two times.

- "New" is signed by cupping the dominant hand. Turn the palm to face you, and strike the back side of the cupped hand along the open palm of the stationary hand.

- Form "year" by making a closed fist with both hands. Circle the dominant fist around the stationary fist until it makes one full rotation. Place the dominant fist to rest on top of the stationary fist.

Halloween

- *Halloween* uses both hands.

- Form the number 2 with each hand. Turn both hands sideways and place the 2s over the eyes as though they were a mask.

- Brush both hands away from the eyes simultaneously.

customs. Or, plan a trip to a new destination. Instead of exchanging gifts, have the trip be the present for all.

If you want to encourage compassion among your children as they get older, consider volunteering at a local food bank or soup kitchen to serve a holiday meal.

Throughout the year write down things for which you are grateful, perhaps items that you have worried about or prayed over and a solution has come about. Or, just record the good blessings in your life as you notice them throughout the year. At Thanksgiving, break open the jar and read aloud all of the

reminders of how thankful you and your family are.

Baking pies? Encourage the kids to become a part of the tradition. Let them create their own recipes while you bake the traditional fare. If the pies actually turn out well, even better!

Thanksgiving

- *Thanksgiving* uses the dominant hand in the letter Q position.

- To form the letter Q, extend the index finger and thumb downward. (Refer to the American Manual Alphabet in Chapter 18.)

- Place the letter Q on the chin. Next, move the hand downward to rest on the chest.

Turkey

- *Turkey* uses the letter Q sign again.

- Place the letter Q on the chin, much like you did for Thanksgiving.

- Move the Q back and forth, representing the red wattle on a turkey.

WINTER HOLIDAYS

Happy holidays! Wish your friends and family the best in the new year

Giving and receiving holiday cards are highlights of the winter season. Seeing how dear family and friends have grown and changed, and all they have done throughout the year, makes receiving holiday cards something to look forward to. Here are some winter holiday card ideas for your family:

Create a collage of memories. Instead of using one picture for the year, show what your family has done all year long by making a collage.

Record all of the cute and funny things your children have done and said throughout the year. Compile the list and put it in the card or on the back of the card. Spread a little holiday humor!

Hanukkah

- Begin with both hands in the number 4 position pointing downward. (Refer to the number list in Chapter 19.)

- Touch the hands together, thumb to thumb and index finger to index finger.

- Rotate the hands around so that the fingertips are now pointing upwards.

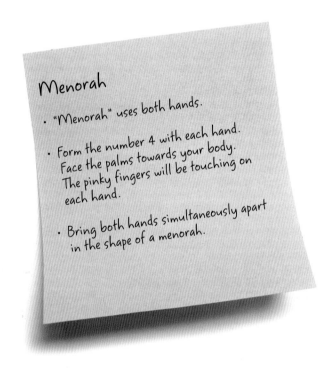

Menorah

- "Menorah" uses both hands.

- Form the number 4 with each hand. Face the palms towards your body. The pinky fingers will be touching on each hand.

- Bring both hands simultaneously apart in the shape of a menorah.

176

Have your child create his own artistic interpretation of a Christmas tree, menorah, or other significant symbol of your faith. Take the design to a local copy center to have cards printed.

Do holidays sneak up on you? Or has your holiday spending already blown the budget? Don't miss the opportunity to reach out to your friends and family. Send an e-card and let them know you're thinking of them.

Surprise your important loved ones with a unique card any time of the year. Upload your pictures onto the computer and create a custom card for any occasion.

New Year

- *New Year* uses both hands.

- Sign *new* by cupping the dominant hand. Turn the palm to face you, and strike the back side of the cupped hand along the open palm of the stationary hand.

- Sign *year* by making a closed fist with both hands. Circle the dominant fist around the stationary fist until it makes one full rotation. Place the dominant fist to rest on top of the stationary fist.

Valentine

- *Valentine* uses both hands.

- Draw a heart shape with the index fingers or with entire hand in the heart region of your chest.

- Have an expression that looks sweet and loving as you sign the word.

177

CHRISTMAS

Feel like the focus on presents diminishes the Christmas spirit? Emphasize giving this holiday season

The Christmas season is an ideal opportunity to teach children to focus not just on what Santa leaves under the tree, but on people and children who are less fortunate. How can you teach a preschooler how to give? Teaching about giving doesn't mean your child has to sacrifice his own gifts. Begin by encouraging compassion for others.

A great way to begin this process is to go to a local mall or large shopping center and participate in an angel tree. Help your child select a child that is similar to him and allow him to pick out the present. If your child begins to feel jealous, remind him that his presents will come at Christmas and this time is about selecting something for someone else.

Christmas: Part One

- *Christmas* begins by forming the letter C with the dominant hand.

- The letter C is formed by cupping the hand slightly with the fingers pressed together. (Refer to the American Manual Alphabet in Chapter 18.)

- Begin with the C in front of you at about mouth level.

Christmas: Part Two

- Next, straighten the arm while opening up the palm of the hand.

- Another version uses the C moving in an arc motion as though it were a Christmas wreath.

Donating to a food bank is a great opportunity to teach giving and can be done all year long. When canned goods are on sale, pick up some extra and talk about what you are doing for others. When your child watches you model a compassionate heart, he will learn compassion.

Too many toys? Before Christmas fills up your already overcrowded playroom or bedrooms, ask your child to help you pick out the toys that she has outgrown or no longer plays with. Talk about how you are not only making room for whatever gifts she might receive, but also helping kids who don't have any toys at all.

See a family in need in the line behind you? Or perhaps a family at your school who has been hit with hard times? Look for ways to help others even with something as simple as just picking up a few groceries or paying the tab at dinner. Generosity doesn't have to cost a bundle.

Tree

- *Tree* uses both hands and arms.

- Place the stationary arm and hand flat and horizontal in front of your body.

- Rest the dominant elbow on the fingertips of the stationary hand.

- Rotate the dominant hand back and forth.

Santa Claus

- *Santa Claus* uses both hands. The sign focuses on the beard of Santa Claus.

- Slightly cup both hands. Place the fingertips of the hands near the chin. The palms face the body.

- Move the hands downwards several times outlining the long and fluffy beard of Santa Claus.

GOOD MANNERS

It's never too early (or late) to introduce good manners

One of the best side effects of signing with your child is that you will find yourself purposefully talking and modeling more. Throughout the dressing, mealtime, playtime, and bedtime routines, take every opportunity to talk and sign using good manners. You can introduce manners to your child when she is an infant.

Though a six-month-old baby may not understand the concept of *thank you* or *please* verbally, through sign the baby will develop a conceptual understanding of these words. For example, if baby wants more, baby learns that by saying *please* through rubbing her hand on her chest in a circular motion she is far more likely to get what she wants. If you model these manners, your baby or child will not just be communicating at an earlier age, but will be practicing manners as well!

Please

- *Please* uses the dominant hand.

- Place the palm of the hand on the middle of the chest area.

- Move the hand in a circular motion several times. Model this word as you play, eat, and ask for things throughout your day.

Thank You

- *Thank you* or *thanks* can use one or both hands.

- Place the hand or hands in a closed number 5 position. Bring the tips of the hand to the tip of the mouth.

- Move the hand or hands away from the mouth several inches.

- To say *you*, point your index finger outward.

Here we will focus on four basic good-manners signs every child should have in his working vocabulary: *please*, *thank you*, *sorry*, and *you're welcome.*

Sorry

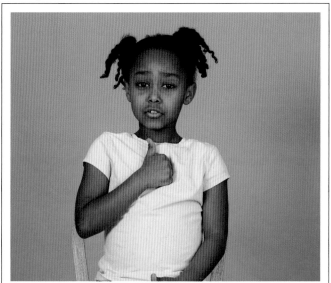

- *Sorry* uses the dominant hand.

- Place the closed fist of the dominant hand in the middle of the chest area.

- Move the hand around in a circular motion, much like *please*.

- Have a look of being authentically sorry when making this sign.

You're Welcome

- *You're welcome* uses the dominant hand.

- Slightly cup the dominant hand and place it several inches away from your mouth.

- Form an arc as you move your hand towards your chest. Nod your head slightly down as you make the sign.

WEATHER

Whatever the weather, using sign language makes communication easier

Sign language is a great tool to use on the go. When you are stuck in rain or snow and need to communicate through car windows or out of voice range, use sign language to say "Grab a coat" or "Bring your gloves." Sign language can be used in any environment. For example:

On the other side of a window: Talk between car windows, doors, or house windows in any weather condition.

Underwater: Swimming or snorkeling? Use signs to talk and communicate.

In line: Whether in an amusement park line or fast food line, take advantage of the ability to communicate with your hands.

Rain

- *Rain* is made using both hands.

- Place both hands at shoulder level with fingers outstretched.

- Move both hands simultaneously downward while wiggling fingers. To differentiate this motion from *snow* the motion should be intense and quick.

Snow

- *Snow* uses both hands.

- Much like rain, begin with both hands at about shoulder level, fingers outstretched.

- Lightly, gently, and slowly flutter the fingers downward as though soft snow is falling.

As your child gets older, despite the ability to communicate verbally, using sign language allows you to communicate anywhere at any time.

Here we will learn four great signs for rainy or wintry weather days: *rain*, *snow*, *mittens* or *gloves*, and *boots*. Weather signs such as these can be introduced to your child at an early age. Just watch for the right context. If it is a rainy day, take advantage of the opportunity to introduce *rain*. Introducing signs in context will help give your child understanding and associations, which will help her retain the sign.

ZOOM

Signing slowing down? Don't be alarmed if your child is suddenly not showing as great an interest in signing and begins to use his enlarging verbal skills. As your child's verbal skills become more proficient it is only normal for him to use his verbal skills more. If you want to keep signing a part of your child's routine, continue to use sign.

Mittens or Gloves

- *Gloves* will use both hands.

- First extend the stationary hand out in a flat number 5 position. Place the dominant hand's fingertips on the tips of the stationary hand.

- Pull the dominant hand back as though it is slipping a glove over the stationary hand.

- Next, repeat the motion with the stationary hand, now slipping the glove onto the dominant hand.

Boots

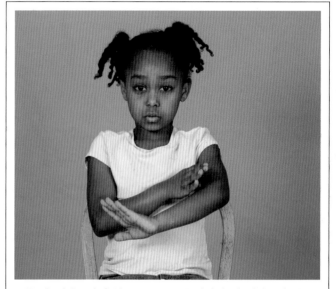

- Use both hands for *boots*.

- Form the letter B with both hands. Fingers will be extended and together with the thumbs in the palms. Position the hands flat, palms facing down.

- Lightly hit both hands together and apart again so that the index fingers and thumbs of both hands touch and come apart. Repeat this motion twice.

BEING RESPONSIBLE

Integrate American Sign Language signs while teaching your child how to be responsible

Here you will learn the signs **put away**, **toy**, and **helper**. As your child grows, these three signs can be used from when she begins to walk, to well into her future. Teaching your child to put away her toys is one way to begin teaching responsibility. What other ways can you help show and teach responsibility to your child?

Do you have a pet? Show your child how to fill and change your pet's water and food bowl.

Your emerging preschooler may not be able to dust every surface, but given a dust rag he can help! Give your child areas to help you clean.

While you are walking in your neighborhood or at the local

Put Away

- Use both hands for this sign.

- Begin by pretending to grasp an object with both hands.

- Simultaneously move both hands as though they are placing something on a shelf.

Toy: Version One

- *Toy* can be signed two different ways.

- This picture demonstrates *toy* in the context of playing with a toy.

- Both hands are formed in the letter Y position with the pinky finger and thumb extended.

- Move both hands back and forth from the wrist. The arms do not move.

park, bring along a trash bag and clean up trash. Talk about the opportunity to help in the community.

Teach your child to make his bed. Okay, it won't be to your standards, but does it have to be? A good place to start is by teaching the child to pull the covers completely straight and flat while still in bed, then to slide out of the bed. Making it fun helps children learn!

Have your child empty his own laundry hamper. It might take a few trips and there might be some spilled socks en route to the laundry room, but you'll be teaching your child

that laundry doesn't magically end up clean in his room. Talk about the process and allow him to be a part of it.

Toy: Version Two

- Alternatively, you can sign *toy* by finger spelling the word: T-O-Y. (Refer to the American Manual Alphabet in Chapter 18.)

- If you choose this method, then you may want to focus on just using the letter T

to represent *toy* until your child is old enough to spell simple words.

- The letter T is formed by placing the thumb in between the index and middle fingers. The remaining fingers are closed.

Helper

- *Helper* uses both hands.

- Create a closed fist with the dominant had.

- Place the stationary hand underneath the fist. Lift both hands simultaneously upward.

185

ACTIVE PLAY

Whatever the age, encouraging movement and activity is healthy for your child

Whether your child is a toddler or a preschooler, he is probably very active. Activity is a great way for your child to release energy, to discover the limits and strengths of his movement, and to stay physically fit. Here we will focus on signs that every child will use: *fall down*, *climb*, *drop*, and *jump*. To an infant or young toddler, introduce these signs in context when baby has an accident, or is attempting to climb on the couch. Or, if baby loves sitting in the jumpy seat in a doorframe or in a springy seat in an exercise saucer, make the sign for *jump* and say "Jump" as you watch your child jump up and down. As your child grows older, continue to use the signs outside or inside as she climbs, jumps, and explores the world around her.

Fall Down

- You will use both hands for this sign.

- Make the number 2 with the dominant hand. Place the tips of the 2 on the flat stationary hand, representing a person standing.

- Next, slide the 2 sideways as though it is falling.

- End the sign with the number 2 resting on the stationary hand, palm facing upwards.

Climb

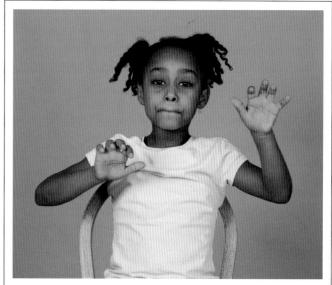

- *Climb* uses both hands.

- Place one hand slightly higher than the other, palms facing outwards.

- Alternately move one hand higher than the other as though you are climbing up a tree or rock wall.

186

If your child expresses interest in playing sports, investigate a recreational or exploratory program in your area. Most communities have programs introducing soccer, basketball, baseball and more, as early as three to four years of age. Just watch your expectations. At this age exposure and having fun are really more important than anything. If your child happens to learn a few fundamental basics, that's even better.

Drop

- *Drop* uses one or two hands.

- Close the fingertips to the thumb.

- Open the fingertips from the thumb as though you are dropping something.

Jump

- *Jump* uses both hands.

- Like in *fall*, make the number 2 sign. Place the tips of the number 2 on the stationary hand as though it is a person standing.

- Move the fingertips off and on the stationary palm as though the person is jumping up and down.

PERSONAL ITEMS
Teach your child about his and others' personal items, and to respect yours

Here we will focus on the signs *glasses*, *Band-Aid*, *beard*, and *belt*. If you wear glasses or sunglasses, chances are your child has already discovered them. Teaching respect for an individual's personal items and space is important. From an early age discourage playing with items such as glasses, television remotes, and keys. Though these coveted items may entertain a fussy toddler temporarily, he is also learning these important items are toys—a message you don't want to teach. While you talk about these personal items, reinforce the message of respecting other people's things. Buy an inexpensive pair of sunglasses your child can wear to be just like you.

Glasses

- The sign for *glasses* can use one or both hands.

- Extend the thumb and index finger while keeping all other fingers closed.

- Place the thumb and index fingers on either side of the eyes representing glasses.

- Keeping the thumb and index finger extended, simultaneously move both hands forward and away from the face. Next place both hands back on the face again, as though the glasses are coming off and on.

Band-Aid

- *Band-Aid* uses both hands.

- Make the letter U with the dominant hand. (Refer to the American Manual Alphabet in Chapter 18.)

- Place the fingertips on the top of the stationary hand. Move the tips backward as though you are placing a Band-Aid on your hand.

Or perhaps you suspect that your child may need a pair of glasses himself. If your child isn't reading or sitting in a classroom yet, what clues can you look for? Schedule an eye exam if you notice that your child squints or rubs his eyes even when he's not sleepy, seems to be sensitive to light, seems awkward or clumsy, wants a book held close to him when you read, produces excessive tears, or always seems to have pus in his eye. If you notice any unusual spots or anything else unexpected about your child's eyes, you should schedule an eye exam for further evaluation.

Beard

- *Beard* uses both hands.

- Cup both hands on either side of the chin.

- Simultaneously move both hands downward in the shape of a beard.

Belt

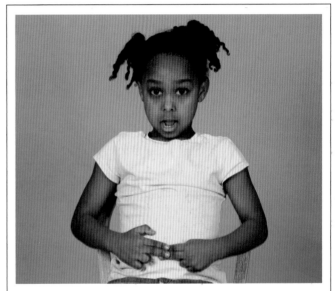

- *Belt* uses both hands.

- Form the letter U with both hands using the index finger and middle finger.

- Place both Us on either side of the waist. Move both hands towards each other simultaneously.

- The motion will end with the fingertips of either U overlapping one another.

SAFETY WORDS
Learning safety and being prepared are musts for any parent

Here we will learn *poison*, *burn*, *shock*, and *fire*—words that are good to know, but that you hope you'll never have cause to use in real life.

To help prevent accidents, educate your child on potential poisons. Household cleaners, car maintenance fluids in the garage, batteries—poisons can come in all forms from solids to liquids and can be in a variety of colors. Teach your child never to put things in her mouth if she doesn't know what it is or whether it is safe to eat or drink.

But what happens if your curious child finds her way into a toxic substance? The first thing you should do after administering first aid is to call poison control (American Association of Poison Control Centers) at 1-800-222-1222, where help is available 24 hours a day, seven days a week. You can even

Poison

- *Poison* uses both hands.

- Position each hand in a bent number 2 position. (Refer to the number list in Chapter 19.)

- Cross both hands over one another at the wrists.

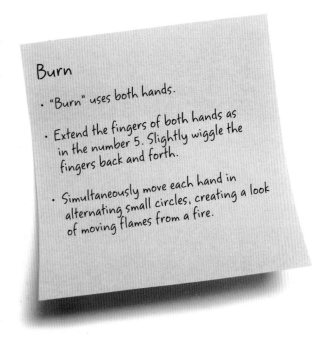

Burn

- "Burn" uses both hands.

- Extend the fingers of both hands as in the number 5. Slightly wiggle the fingers back and forth.

- Simultaneously move each hand in alternating small circles, creating a look of moving flames from a fire.

call this number to receive free stickers to post near phones for babysitters or in times of emergency, or to find the closest poison center near you. Calling poison control is essential because they will determine if an ambulance is needed (and will call one for you) and they can walk you through what you need to look for, preventing unneeded runs to the emergency room. Poison control is an invaluable source of support and information.

ZOOM

It's hard for a young child to wrap her head around the danger of poisons or what they can do to her. Help explain poisons by telling your child they can be in any form—something to drink, something she can chew, even something she can smell—and can make her sick. Putting the poison in concrete, understandable terms will help your child avoid new and potentially dangerous substances.

Shock

- *Shock* uses both hands.

- Place both hands at shoulder level, slightly cupped and with fingers apart.

- Both palms face the ground.

- Move both hands back and forth slightly with great intensity.

- Be sure your face and tone are conveying a sense of urgency and shock.

Fire

- *Fire* uses both hands.

- Much like burn, both hands will be in the number 5 position with the palms facing your body.

- Wiggle the fingers slightly back and forth while moving both hands simultaneously upward.

- The upward movement indicates something burning up.

191

MEALS
Breakfast, lunch, and dinner are core elements of any child's day

Looking for lunch? Here you will teach your child the signs for **breakfast**, **lunch**, and **dinner**. You began with learning *eat* in the very beginning of Chapter 1. Here you will build upon that generic word to focus specifically on the meal. Because your child's day is in large part based around these three meals, take the time to learn and use these signs.

Breakfast is an important start to every person's day. Even if your child isn't a big morning eater, make sure she gets the day started even with something small like yogurt, fruit, or a piece of whole-grain toast. Keeping snacks confined to a designated time will help your child be hungry for lunch and dinner. Eating at about the same time every day not only helps your child feel consistency in the day and thus more control, it also helps your child make it to mealtime. If a child

Breakfast

- *Breakfast* is made using one hand.

- Form the letter B with the dominant hand. The letter B uses all four fingers extended with the thumb closed into the palm.

- Place the index finger of the dominant hand in the middle of the mouth and move it downwards until the fingertips are just below the chin.

- Repeat the motion one time.

Lunch: Part One

This is the sign for "eat"

- Like *breakfast*, lunch is also made up of two signs—*eat* and *noon*.

- For *eat*, close the fingertips to the thumb. Place the tips of the hands close to the mouth.

- You should look like you are putting food in your mouth.

doesn't know when dinner is coming, snacking to quell the hunger pains is more likely.

Remember that eating everything on the plate isn't as important as ending the day with a balanced diet. If your child loads up on milk and yogurt at breakfast, don't offer cheese at lunch. Instead, try to balance the meal with proteins and carbohydrates. Balance, listening to your child when he says he is full, and being active will help create lifelong healthy eating habits.

This position mimics the hands of a clock being straight up at noon.

Lunch: Part Two

- *Noon* uses both hands and arms.

- The stationary arm and hand are flat and horizontal.

- The dominant elbow rests on the stationary hand. The hand is flat and straight.

Dinner

- *Dinner* uses the dominant hand in a letter D position.

- Form the letter D by extending the index finger with all other fingers closed in an O. (Refer to the Ameri-can Manual Alphabet in Chapter 18.)

- Place the D on the mouth with fingertips on the lips. Move the D to and away from the lips several times.

TABLE TALK

Want to learn signs for around the table? *Swallow*, *bite*, *table*, and *plate* will help expand your table talk

Eating together as a family, whatever your family may look like, is a great togetherness activity for all. Whether your meal is at a restaurant, at the park, or around your kitchen table, what is important is that it is a time for everyone to come together and talk. Little family traditions can be created around mealtime. For example, every Tuesday can be a make-your-own-

taco night. Or, you might take turns going around the table with each person stating the high point and low point of their day. Not only will this allow mom and dad to catch up on what happened at school or daycare, but it ensures all have a place to be heard, to feel a part of a family, and to reconnect with one another despite being apart all day.

Swallow

- *Swallow* uses one hand.

- Form the number 1 with the dominant hand. (Refer to the number list in Chapter 19.)

- Place the tip of the finger at the top of your throat.

- Trace the finger down the length of the neck.

- *Swallow* is similar to *thirsty*, but with only one finger and without the facial expression and tone of desperation that accompanies the sign.

Bite

- *Bite* uses one hand.

- Bring the dominant hand near the mouth as though it were a sandwich and then make the biting motion.

- Pretend to take a bite out of an imaginary sandwich.

While making mealtime fun helps foster closeness, don't forget basic table manners and safety precautions. Make sure your child is seated and chews his food properly before swallowing. If your child is choking he won't be able to cough or talk. If your child can make sound, he is okay. Choking is silent. Learn how to safely perform the Heimlich maneuver before your child ever needs it. Be prepared in case of an emergency.

Table

- *Table* uses both hands and arms.

- Place the dominant arm on top of the stationary arm. Both arms should be shoulder level, horizontal, palms facing the ground.

- Tap the dominant palm on and off the stationary elbow. The arms should resemble a table top.

Plate

- *Plate* uses both hands.

- Begin with both middle fingers touching.

- Pull both hands apart to form a circle, meeting again at the inside of the wrist. Both wrists will touch.

DELICIOUS FRUITS
Yummy and nutritious snacks for added health benefits

Eating fruit provides so many wonderful health benefits for your child. Here we will learn the signs for *grapes*, *cherry*, *pineapple*, and *cantaloupe*, all of which provide remarkable health benefits. Red grapes contain strong antioxidants, one of which is resveratrol, which has been shown to help reduce cancer and cardiovascular risk. Grapes have also been shown to reduce blood pressure after the ingestion of salty foods.

Like grapes, cherries are also high in antioxidants, which help fight free radicals in your body. Cherries are a fat free, low calorie sweet treat that can easily be served as a dessert after a meal, or as a side with lunch or dinner.

Watch out for juice. While it sounds healthy, juice is loaded with sugar. Limit juice to just one serving per day.

Have the sniffles? Rather than reaching for the orange juice,

Grapes

- *Grapes* uses both hands.

- Place the stationary hand with the palm facing the ground. The hand should be bent at the wrist so it is hanging loosely, much like a bunch of grapes hanging off a vine.

- Next, cup the dominant hand and place it on the stationary hand. Move the hand on and off the hand in various places on the stationary hand as though it is grasping clusters of grapes off of a vine.

Cherry

- *Cherry* uses both hands.

- Extend the stationary pinky finger outward while all other fingers remain closed.

- The dominant hand will grasp the end of the pinky finger with all fingers tightened around it.

- From the wrist, twist the dominant hand back and forth.

consider pineapple or pineapple juice for a great source of vitamin C. Pineapple also is loaded with calcium and manganese important for healthy bone building.

Pineapple

- Form the letter P with the dominant hand.

- The letter P uses the index and middle finger extended with the thumb resting between both fingers. All other fingers are closed.

- Place the P with fingertips resting on the cheek.

- From the wrist, twist the P back and forth.

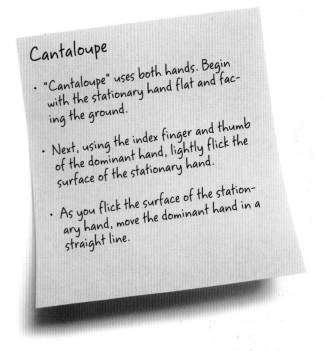

Cantaloupe

- "Cantaloupe" uses both hands. Begin with the stationary hand flat and facing the ground.

- Next, using the index finger and thumb of the dominant hand, lightly flick the surface of the stationary hand.

- As you flick the surface of the stationary hand, move the dominant hand in a straight line.

EATING OUT
Have an enjoyable meal instead of embarrassing moments

Going out to eat with family for burgers or a pizza can be a great reprieve from the kitchen. Make your meal a fun family outing rather than a hiding-under-the-table-from-embarrassment experience.

Do your homework before you head out the door. Don't go to a restaurant to which you've never been, or one that is notoriously slow; save those for an adults-only night. Pick a restaurant that you know is child-friendly, has a good kids' menu, and has fairly fast service. Though you may think your child is grown up enough for a more adult establishment, if your child has a meltdown, the other diners will pay the price. Consider the other restaurant guests as well.

Second, don't arrive when your child's hunger is in full swing. If your child is too hungry, waiting any amount of time

Restaurant

- *Restaurant* uses only one hand.

- Form the letter R by crossing the middle finger over the index finger. (Refer to the American Manual Alphabet in Chapter 18.)

- Place the R on one side of the mouth, then place it on the other side of the mouth.

Pizza

- *Pizza* can be signed two different ways.

- Pretend to hold an entire piece of pizza and make the motion of taking a bite.

- Or, form the letter P sign and draw out the letter Z in the space in front of you with the P.

for food to arrive will be painful for all. In a bind, ask for crackers or rolls, though be careful not to let your child fill up on these before the meal.

Third, encourage seat sitting by bringing along crayons and activity books. Wandering children can be distracting and dangerous even in the most child-friendly restaurants. Help teach your child table manners by setting expectations of staying at the table. Use the opportunity to remind the children that napkins belong on the lap, that lips are closed when eating, and that we don't talk with our mouths full.

And finally, eating out isn't the time to force new foods or to be rigid. Once in a while it is okay for your child to have fried chicken tenders and French fries. Take the opportunity to enjoy the meal as a family and savor the break from the kitchen.

Hamburger

- *Hamburger* uses both hands.

- Begin with one hand cupped on top of the other.

- Next switch hands so the opposite hand is now on top.

Hot Dog

- *Hot dog* uses both hands.

- As you make this sign, it will look like you are forming sausage links.

- Begin with closed fists in the letter S position with thumbs resting across the fingers.

- Starting with the fists close together, move the hands away from each other while opening the hands into the letter C position and closing them back to letter S. Repeat this several times.

BREAKFAST
Have a healthy start to your day

Beyond being fulfilling and nutritious, breakfast has been shown to have pretty profound effects on overall health. Breakfast is thought to jump-start your metabolism for the day. For your emerging student, eating breakfast has proven to result in higher standardized test scores. A full tummy reduces distraction, allows a child to focus on something other than hunger, and provides a source of continued energy. People who skip breakfast also tend to bank up on calories later. Ironically, skipping breakfast can lead to a higher calorie count for the day.

Nutritionally, breakfast provides important vitamins and minerals that may be overlooked with higher calorie and fatty foods eaten later in the day. Help encourage your child to get in the breakfast habit now.

Egg

- *Egg* uses both hands.

- Both hands will form the letter H using the index and middle finger. (Refer to the American Manual Alphabet in Chapter 18.)

- Place the dominant middle finger on top of the other middle finger.

- Move both hands downward and outward simultaneously.

Cereal

- *Cereal* uses both hands.

- Hold the stationary hand flat, palm facing upward to symbolize the cereal bowl.

- Next, use the dominant hand to scoop cereal towards the mouth. This motion should look like you're eating a bowl of cereal.

Is your morning already chaotic? Plan the night before what you will eat for breakfast. Wake up a few minutes earlier to ensure both you and your child receive the healthy breakfast you need and deserve! Breakfast doesn't have to be bacon and eggs or cereal. Granola, granola bars, yogurt, whole grain toast or bagels, breakfast bars, whole grain waffles, fruit mixed with yogurt or in cereal, breakfast burritos, and English muffins are good ideas to help get you started. By giving yourself and your child the gift of a regular and consistent breakfast, you'll reap the rewards of increased energy in the morning and feeling less hungry later in the day.

Here we will focus on four breakfast basics: *egg*, *cereal*, *butter*, and *bacon*. Use these signs as you help prepare your body and breakfast for a great day!

Butter

- *Butter* uses both hands. The motion will look somewhat like spreading butter on a piece of toast.

- The stationary hand is flat, palm facing up.

- Extend the index and middle finger close together, keeping the other fingers closed.

- Brush the extended fingers along the open palm.

Bacon

- *Bacon* uses both hands.

- Each hand extends the index finger and middle finger. All other fingers will be closed.

- Begin with both hands touching at the fingertips.

- Pull the hands away from each other.

- As the hands pull away from one another, slightly wiggle the index and middle fingers back and forth.

201

DESSERT
How much sugar is too much for your child?

Sugar is hidden in many of our common foods. In fact, before we even reach for dessert, chances are we've ingested far more sugar than our body ever needs. Added sugars can be found in everyday items like cereals, yogurt, a cinnamon raisin bagel, muffins, spaghetti sauce, and so much more. Ingesting too much sugar is harmful because it is loaded with calories and delivers zero nutritional benefits. Sugary

sodas, especially for children, can dramatically increase sugar consumption, ultimately contributing to unnecessary weight gain. If your child is a less-than-thorough brusher, then you also have to worry about potential tooth decay. So, make some little adjustments in the day so your sugar calories can be spent on the occasional dessert and not on hidden sugars throughout the day.

Dessert

- *Dessert* uses both hands.

- Form the letter D with both hands. (Refer to the American Manual Alphabet in Chapter 18.)

- Bring both hands together and apart again. Repeat this motion two or three times.

Delicious

- *Delicious* uses one hand.

- Begin with the middle finger extended towards the mouth as though you have just sampled something.

- Bring the finger away from the mouth and swipe it against the thumb.

- Make an expression that reflects something tasty!

202

Instead of serving sugar-added cereals, reach for toasted oat cereal or whole grain cereals with no added sugars. These cereals are still delicious and you've just saved teaspoons of added sugar. Look at the label and search for cereals that offer less than one teaspoon, or four grams, per serving. If your child is already addicted to a high-sugar cereal, consider mixing it half and half with another low-sugar cereal. Your child won't be giving up his favorite cereal cold turkey, and you'll still dramatically cut sugar consumption.

Instead of a muffin loaded in sugar, reach for whole grain toast, bagel chips, or whole grain bagels.

Instead of sugar-filled popsicles, offer popsicles made from fruit. Fruit, while containing natural sugars, provides nutritional benefits as well. Both taste great, so why not reach for the treat that offers more for your body than sugar?

In any case, sugar should always be consumed in moderation. Your child's diet should never be so dominated by sugar that it leaves little room for healthy nutritional choices.

Popsicle

- Pretend to hold a popsicle in the dominant hand.

- Act as though you are licking or eating a popsicle.

- Have an expression or tone that indicates you are eating something delicious.

Chocolate

- *Chocolate* uses both hands.

- The stationary hand will be facing the ground.

- Form the letter C with the dominant hand and rest it on the stationary hand.

- Move the C in two circles moving away from the stationary hand and resting again on the hand.

AMERICAN MANUAL ALPHABET
Letters form the foundation of many ASL signs

The American Manual Alphabet is the backbone of American Sign Language, the native language of the deaf community. Often, those who want to learn ASL in order to communicate with the deaf begin here. Obviously, having a working knowledge of the letters enables anyone to finger spell and have basic communication with the deaf.

You may have already begun to pick up a few important letters as you've learned signs for your child. As you've probably noticed, many signs include a letter as a foundation of the sign. Learning the alphabet is a great idea if you want to expand your knowledge of ASL or if you just want to have visual reinforcement of the alphabet as you teach your child his letters. In baby sign language, the primary goal is to communicate with your child, especially in the earliest months. Because your child will not be ready to grasp the alphabet nor spelling until the preschool years, don't feel like you need to have a good grasp of the alphabet before you learn other signs.

Learning the American Manual Alphabet is pretty easy, especially if you've already begun to sign with your child. Sign the letters of the alphabet with your dominant hand. If you are right-handed your dominant hand is the right hand. If you are left-handed, sign with your left.

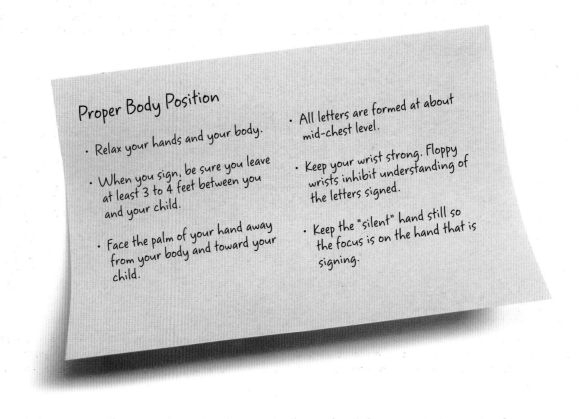

Proper Body Position

- Relax your hands and your body.

- When you sign, be sure you leave at least 3 to 4 feet between you and your child.

- Face the palm of your hand away from your body and toward your child.

- All letters are formed at about mid-chest level.

- Keep your wrist strong. Floppy wrists inhibit understanding of the letters signed.

- Keep the "silent" hand still so the focus is on the hand that is signing.

The Letter A

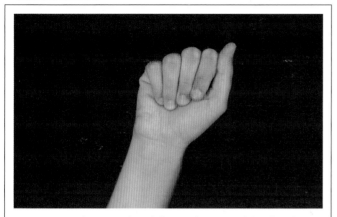

- Using your dominant hand, form a fist. Extend the thumb upwards and press it tightly against the closed fingers of the fist. The remaining fingers will be folded down and touching.

The Letter B

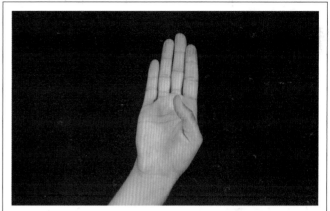

- Extend all four fingers straight up, while pressing the thumb across the center of the palm. There should be no spaces between any of the fingers. Remember to face the palm away from your body.

The Letter C

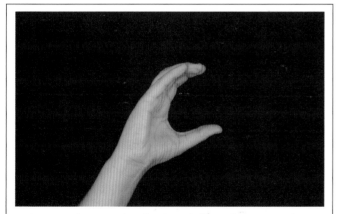

- Cup your dominant hand to form a shape that mimics the letter C in written English. The curved fingers of the hand will be touching with no spaces between them. Hold your wrist still as you sign.

The Letter D

- Using your dominant hand, extend the index finger straight up. The middle finger and thumb will touch forming a circle, resembling a lowercase D. The remaining fingers are closed.

The Letter E

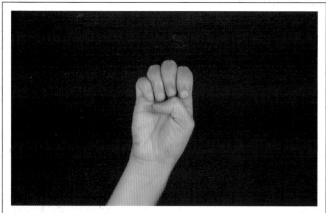

- Using your dominant hand, form the letter E by folding the thumb across the palm of the hand. All other fingers will be folded and resting on top of the thumb.

The Letter F

- Touch the index finger and thumb together to form a circle. Extend the remaining three fingers. There should be space in between the extended fingers.

The Letter G

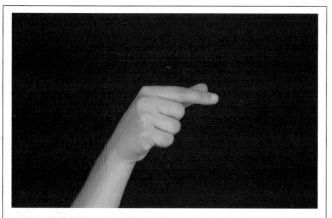

- Extend the thumb and index finger in a horizontal position. The remaining three fingers will be closed. The index finger will be facing away from your body while the thumb faces your body.

The Letter H

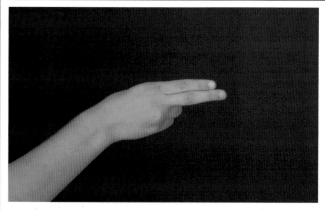

- Extend the index and middle finger out while folding in the thumb, ring, and pinky fingers. The index and middle finger will be horizontal with no space between them.

The Letter I

- I is simple! Close in all fingers except the pinky finger. Extend the pinky finger straight. To say *I* as a pronoun, place the thumb side of the fist on the center of the chest.

The Letter J

- Begin J with your hand in the letter I position, pinky extended. Next, curve your pinky in a downward curved motion so the pinky finishes directly underneath your wrist.

The Letter K

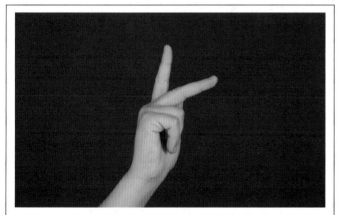

- Form the letter K by extending the middle and index fingers. Place the thumb between the extended fingers. The remaining fingers are closed. The fingers should look much like the written K.

The Letter L

- Extend the thumb to the side and the index finger straight. Fold the remaining three fingers. Though the L does mirror the written L, use your left hand if that is your dominant hand.

The Letter M

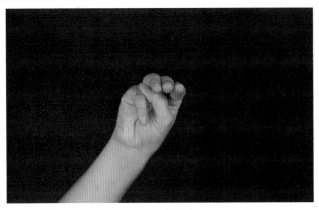

- The most important element of the letter M is where to place the thumb. Make sure to place the thumb between the pinky finger and ring finger.

The Letter N

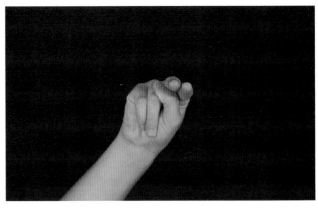

- Much like the letter M, all fingers are folded. However, now place the thumb between the middle and ring fingers. Remember, M is three fingers over, and N is two.

The Letter O

- Letter O is formed by closing all the fingers to touch the thumb. Curve the palm so it makes a round shape. The thumb and fingers will face away from your body.

The Letter P

- Letter P is essentially an upside down K. Rest the thumb between the middle and index fingers. Point the hand downward. To make it easy, first form K and then point it downward.

The Letter Q

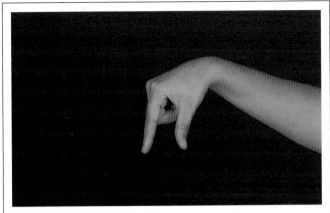

- The letter Q uses the index finger and the thumb. Point both downward while keeping the remaining fingers closed in. The palm will be facing away from your body.

The Letter R

- If you know how to cross your fingers for good luck, then you know how to form the letter R. Simply cross the middle finger over the index finger.

The Letter S

- The letter S and the letter A can be easily confused. Watch your thumb placement here to be sure you are signing S. Form a closed fist with the thumb resting in front of the closed fingers.

The Letter T

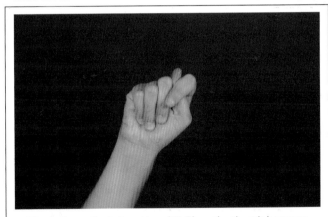

- T is similar to the letters M and N. Place the thumb between the index finger and middle finger with all other fingers folded. Make sure the thumb is in the right spot to avoid saying the wrong letter!

The Letter U

- U resembles the written letter U with the index and middle finger extended upwards. All other fingers will be closed. Do not space the fingers apart, or you will be forming the letter V.

The Letter V

- Much like the letter U, V also extends the index and middle finger. Leave enough space between the two fingers to resemble a V-like shape. This is also the sign for the number 2.

The Letter W

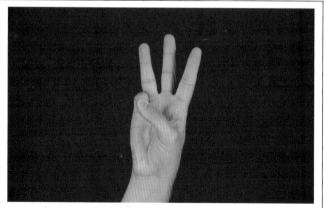

- The letter W looks much like what popular culture uses for the number 3, extending out the index, middle, and ring fingers. In ASL, this is also the sign for the number 6.

The Letter X

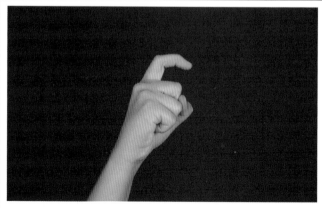

- X uses only the index finger with all other fingers in a closed fist. Bend the index finger at both joints. Be sure the finger is bent in both places to form a clear letter.

The Letter Y

- Simply extend the pinky finger and the thumb to form the letter Y. All other fingers will be closed. Remember to hold your hand and arm still to aid understanding.

The Letter Z

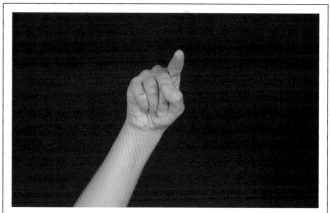

- Using your index finger, write the letter Z in the air. This easy-to-sign letter is fun to teach your child, so don't be afraid to have fun while you practice your alphabet skills.

The American Manual Alphabet helps reinforce alphabetic principles

Learning the alphabet is a fundamental pre-reading skill. When children are aware of the letters, letter sounds, and letter shapes, they are equipped with the basic skills needed to begin learning and reading words. The American Manual Alphabet can be a valuable tool to help reinforce letter awareness. Not only will your child understand that sounds correspond with written letters, but they can also correspond with letter shapes by hand. For example, have your child finger spell his name. Or, have your child locate the beginning, middle, or ending sound of a word and then form the corresponding letter. Sound out simple words and have your child finger spell the sounds. The American Manual Alphabet can be a valuable asset to mastering the alphabet and setting the foundation for excellent reading skills.

Not only will the AMA help your emerging reader, but your child can potentially develop a lifelong foreign language skill. Because the AMA is the backbone of American Sign Language, the alphabet coupled with other signs your child has learned will provide a great ASL foundation. American Sign Language is a recognized foreign language and ranks as the third most spoken language behind English and Spanish in the United States.

NUMBERS

Count to 100 using just one hand

Counting and learning one-to-one correspondence is the foundation for meaningful math. Understanding the conceptual meaning of quantity, order, and sequence help little people build a strong foundation for future math skills. These basic math principles bring order and understanding to a preschooler's world. When a preschooler is able to count how many snacks, blocks, or crayons, he is able not only to master a skill, but to feel a sense of control over his environment. Learning to count in American Sign Language is another tool to help reinforce your child's math skills.

Beyond reinforcing math skills, being able to communicate numbers by hand can help your child easily communicate to you in a variety of settings. For example, in a busy restaurant your child can tell you how many; in an emergency, 9-1-1 can be easily communicated; or you can send a 1-2-3 warning in a quiet setting. Beyond math, numbers have practical application every day, so learn how to use these numbers in your world.

Number 1

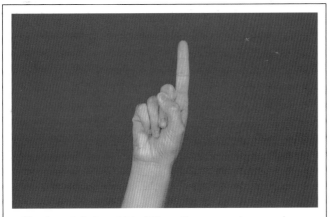

- Numbers 1, 2, 4, and 5 in ASL are the same as how you have probably said these numbers your whole life. For one, simply extend the index finger up.

Number 2

- The ASL number 2 and the ASL letter V are the same sign. Form 2 by extending the index and middle finger. Be sure to leave space between these fingers.

Number 3

- The ASL 3 is different than the popular-culture version of number 3, which is the ASL number 6. To sign 3, extend the thumb, index, and middle fingers, leaving space between them.

Number 4

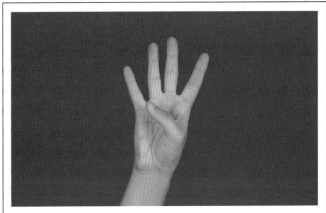

- Sign the ASL 4 just as you would when counting on your fingers. Extend all four fingers with spaces between them, while the thumb rests in the palm of the hand.

Number 5

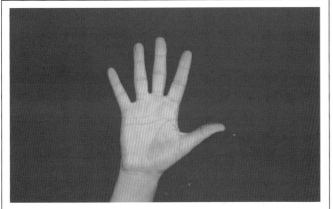

- Like 1, 2, and 4, the number 5 in ASL is the same as popular culture. Extend all five fingers outward with spaces between them. Remember not to shake too much from the wrist or elbow.

Number 6

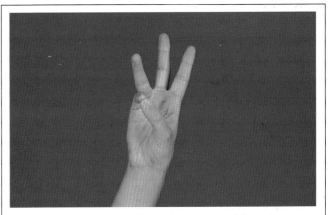

- The ASL number 6 is made just how you would say the number 3 in popular culture. Extend the middle three fingers while closing the pinky and thumb together.

Number 7

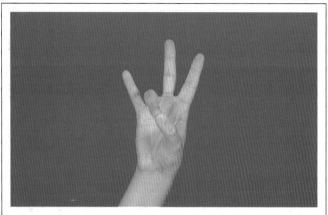

- To form the ASL number 7, bring the ring finger and thumb together. All other fingers will be extended with spaces between them. You don't even need the other hand to count!

Number 8

- The ASL 8 uses the middle finger and the thumb. Bring both to touch. All other fingers will be extended straight with space between them. Don't confuse fingers or you will be saying a different number.

Number 9

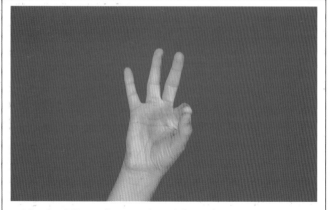

- Like the ASL number 7 and 8, 9 follows this same pattern. The index finger and thumb will touch while all other fingers are extended. Practice counting from 6 to 9 for practice and retention.

Number 10

- The number 10 uses the thumb and a rotation of the wrist. Begin the motion with the thumb sideways. Rotate from the wrist upwards quickly.

Number 11

- The number 11 uses the index finger and thumb with the other fingers closed in a fist. Begin with the nail of the index finger just below the thumb and then quickly flick it outward.

Number 12

- The ASL 12 is much like the number 11, but this time use the index and middle finger. Bring both fingers to the thumb and then quickly flick them forward.

Number 13

- Begin the ASL 13 with the ASL number 3. Face the palm towards your body, then fold the index finger and middle finger toward the palm back and forth two times.

Number 14

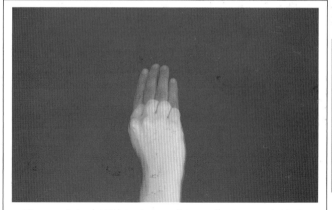

- The number 14 is formed using the number 4. Face the palm of the hand towards your body. Fold the fingers back and forth over the thumb two times.

Number 15

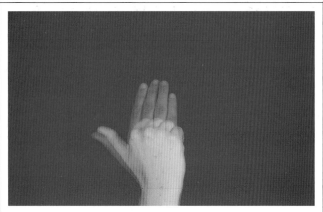

- Begin the ASL 15 by forming the number 5. Face the palm of the hand towards your body. Fold the four fingers back and forth quickly two times.

Number 16

- Begin 16 with the hand in the letter A position, with a closed fist and thumb to the side. Next, form the ASL number 6 with the middle three fingers extended.

Number 17

- First, begin 17 with the hand in the ASL letter A position with a closed fist and thumb to the side. Next, form the ASL number 7 with the ring finger and thumb touching.

Number 18

- Begin in the letter A position with a closed fist and thumb to the side. Next, form the number 8 by touching the middle finger and thumb together with all other fingers extended.

Number 19

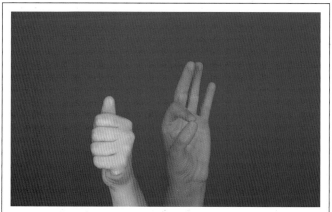

- Like 16, 17, and 18, the ASL number 19 will follow the same pattern. First form the letter A. Next form the number 9 with the index finger and thumb touching with the remaining fingers extended.

Number 20

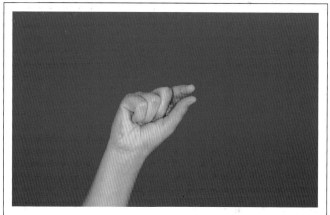

- Close the index finger and thumb together. Move the fingers apart and together again several times. The remaining fingers will be in a closed fist.

Larger Numbers

Are you getting the hang of counting large numbers with your hands? Practice counting 1 to 10 and try to go increasingly faster to help refine your finger fluidity. To sign a number like 34, first sign the 3, and beside where you signed the 3, sign the number 4.

Higher denominations are easy to sign. To sign a number in the thousand range, first sign the number, then the thousand sign by placing the fingertips of the dominant hand onto the open palm of the stationary hand. So to say 8,000 you would first sign 8, then the thousand sign. To say 8,352, the sign would

be made up of 8, thousand sign, 3, hundred sign, 5, then 2. To say a number in the million range, make the same sign as thousand but tap the fingertips to the hand twice with the second tap being placed slightly higher on the palm.

When signing numbers and letters it is especially important to be aware of how much your hand or arm is moving. A steady hand and arm will be easier to understand. Numbers and letters are always signed at about mid-chest level. Remember not to be too close to the person to whom you are signing.

Number 30

- To form 30, simply make the ASL 3 using the index and middle finger and thumb. After forming the *3*, quickly bring in those three fingers to form a 0 shape while your ring finger and pinky finger remain closed in.

Number 40

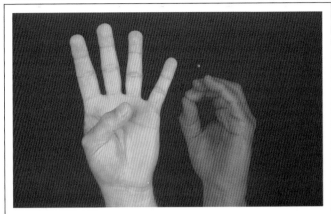

- Begin 40 with the number 4. The four fingers will be extended with spaces between the fingers. The thumb will be pressed against the palm. Next, form the number 0.

Number 50

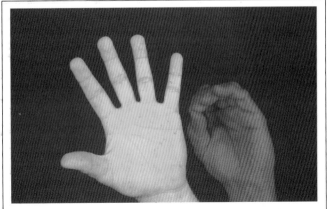

- First, form the number 5, extending all five fingers with spaces between all. The palm of the hand will be facing away from your body. Second, form the number 0.

Number 60

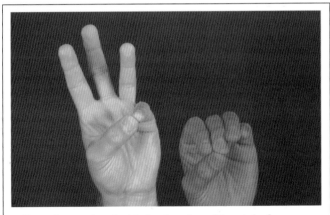

- Form the number 6 with the thumb and the pinky finger touching. The remaining three fingers will be extended straight with spaces between each finger. Next form the number 0.

Number 70

- Begin by forming the number 7 using the ring finger and thumb pressed together. All other fingers will be extended. Next, form the number 0.

Number 80

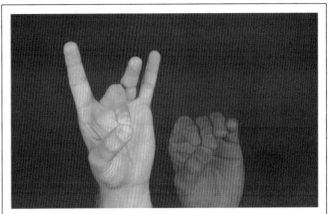

- Form number 80 by making the number 8 with middle finger and thumb touching, followed by the number 0. To sign a number in the 80 range, begin with 8, then the next number. For example, 82 would be 8 then 2.

Number 90

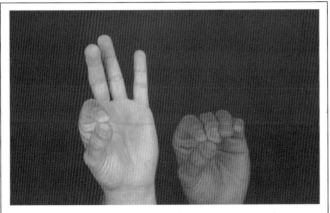

- The number 90 begins with the number 9 using the index finger and thumb. All other fingers are extended. Next, form 0 by closing all fingers together. Your hand should be at mid-chest level.

Number 100

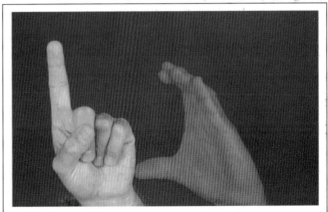

- The sign for 100 is a compound sign. First, form the number 1. Extend the index finger straight while all other fingers are closed. Next, form the letter C by cupping the hand.

- To say 200, say the number 2 then the hundred sign and so on.

FINGER PLAY FUN

Finger play is fun and easy. As your child begins to mimic motions back to you, he is actually honing his manual dexterity skills. And putting words to music in conjunction with hand movements helps aid memory retention. Your child is more likely to recall rhymes put to music and motion. So, sing, be silly and know that this fun play is educational too!

"Itsy Bitsy Spider"
Itsy bitsy spider went up the water spout
(Make climbing motions with fingers)
Down came the rain
(Wiggle fingers down from head to waist)
And washed the spider out
(Throw arms to sides)
Out came the sun and dried up all the rain
(Raise hands above head, make circle for sun)
Now the itsy bitsy spider
Went up the spout again
(Climb fingers again)

"I'm a Little Teapot"
I'm a little teapot
Short and stout
Here is my handle
(Place one hand on hip with elbow out)
Here is my spout
(Extend other hand outward)
When I get all steamed up,
Hear me shout!
Tip me over and pour me out!
(Lean over to side and tip arm like a spout)

"Where is Thumbkin?"

"Where is Thumbkin" teaches cause and effect. It also teaches your child about the fingers on her hand, and how to have a good introduction. The song begins with each thumb making its acquaintance and ends with the entire hand (or family) saying hello and goodbye.

Where is Thumbkin?
Where is Thumbkin?
Here I am
(Extend right thumb in front of body)
Here I am
(Extend left thumb in front of body)
How are you this morning?
Very well, I thank you
(Wiggle both thumbs as though talking)
Run away
(Hide right hand behind back)
Run away
(Hide left hand behind back)

Repeat same lyrics and motions using your index, middle, ring, and pinky fingers and naming them as follows:
Index finger: "Where is pointer?"
Middle finger: "Where is tall man?"
Ring finger: "Where is ring man?"
Pinky finger: "Where is pinky?"

ZOOM

Songs like "Where is Thumbkin" and "Head and Shoulders" help teach your child order and sequence. "Thumbkin" teaches children the various fingers, increasing dexterity by discovering how to hold each finger independently. With "Head and Shoulders" your child is learning sequence in the song as well as parts of the body!

"Head & Shoulders"

This get-up-and-move-your-body song not only teaches your child the parts of the body, it also uses the entire body in movement and motion. You'll begin in a standing position, touching your head, shoulders, knees, toes, eyes, ears, mouth, and finally the nose.

Head and shoulders, knees and toes, knees and toes
Head and shoulders, knees and toes, knees and toes
And eyes, and ears, and mouth, and nose
Head and shoulders, knees and toes, knees and toes

GREEN ● LIGHT

Did you know that rhyming helps your child read? Through rhyming your child is introduced to language families such as cat, sat, and mat. Rhyming also helps your child listen and be aware of different sound patterns and experiment with those sounds. This phonetic awareness will help your child with his future reading and writing skills. Using voice inflection and animation with the rhymes also helps your child later when he begins to read aloud.

RESOURCES

"Baby Bumblebee"

I'm bringing home a baby bumblebee!
Won't my Mommy be so proud of me!
(Cup both hands together and move back and forth)

I'm bringing home a baby bumblebee.
 Ouch! It stung me!
(Shake hands as if just stung)

I'm squishing up the baby bumblebee.
 Won't my mommy be so proud of me?
(Pretend to squish bee between palms of hands)

I'm squishing up a baby bumblebee.
 Ooh! It's yucky!
(Open up hands to look at the yucky mess)

I'm wiping off the baby bumblebee.
 Won't my mommy be so proud of me?
(Wipe hands on shirt or pants)

I'm wiping off the baby bumblebee.
 Now my mommy won't be mad at me!
(Hold hands up to show they are clean)

GREEN ● LIGHT

Find yourself saying "Ssshhhh" or "Quiet" all the time? In this fun finger play song, let your child cut loose and be a little loud. Each verse gives a child an opportunity to express a new emotion. From excitement to surprise to disgust, "Baby Bumblebee" gives your child a fun way to explore how different emotions feel and look. This time is about having fun, not reprimands, so try not to worry about the noise level. Relax a little and enjoy being silly and animated with your child.

"Wheels on the Bus"

The wheels on the bus go round and round
Round and round, round and round
The wheels on the bus go round and round
All through the town
(Roll hands over one another or create large circles with index finger)

The wipers on the bus go "Swish, swish, swish
Swish, swish, swish, swish, swish, swish"
The wipers on the bus go "Swish, swish, swish"
All through the town
(Move both arms together emulating the swish of a windshield wiper)

The door on the bus goes open and shut
Open and shut, open and shut
The door on the bus goes open and shut
All through the town
(Cover eyes and face with both hands for shut, and uncover hands and face for open)

The horn on the bus goes "Beep, beep, beep
Beep, beep, beep, beep, beep, beep"
The horn on the bus goes "Beep, beep, beep"
All through the town
(Pretend to honk horn)

The baby on the bus says, "Wah, wah, wah! Wah, wah, wah
wah, wah, wah!
The baby on the bus says, "Wah, wah, wah!"
All through the town
*(Put both fists in front of eyes and pretend to rub them back
and forth)*

The people on the bus say, "Shh, shh, shh,
Shh, shh, shh, shh, shh, shh"
The people on the bus say, "Shh, shh, shh,"
All through the town
(Make the shh sign by placing the index finger in front of lips)

The mommy and the daddy say, "I love you,
I love you, I love you."
The mommy and daddy say, "I love you"
All through the town
*(Make the I love you sign using the thumb, index finger,
and pinky finger)*

Other verses:
The people on the bus go up and down.
The driver on the bus says, "Move on back!"
The signals on the bus go blink, blink, blink.
The motor on the bus goes zoom, zoom, zoom.

Using finger play songs and rhymes helps your child improve his listening skills. Because your child will want to join in and sing along, he will be working his listening skills to hear and recite what was said.

"If You're Happy and You Know It"

This song encourages your child to creatively use his body while experimenting with emotion and movement. To change it up a little bit, change the lyrics to what to do when sad (perhaps crying a tear), or saying "hooray." Don't be afraid to make these songs your own by adding your own twist!

If you're happy and you know it,
Clap your hands.
(Clap hands twice)

If you're happy and you know it,
Clap your hands.
(Clap hands twice)

If you're happy and you know it,
Then your hands will surely show it.
If you're happy and you know it,
Clap your hands.
(Clap hands twice)

If you're happy and you know it,
Stomp your feet.
(Stomp foot twice)

If you're happy and you know it,
Stomp your feet.
(Stomp foot twice)

If you're happy and you know it,
Then your feet will surely show it
If you're happy and you know it,
Stomp your feet.
(Stomp foot twice)

If you're happy and you know it,
Nod your head.
(Nod head)

If you're happy and you know it,
Nod your head.
(Nod head)

If you're happy and you know it,
Then your head will surely show it.
If you're happy and you know it,
Nod your head.
(Nod head)

If you're happy and you know it,
Do all three.
(Clap hands, stomp feet, and nod head)

If you're happy and you know it,
Do all three.
(Clap hands, stomp feet, and nod head)

If you're happy and you know it,
Then your face will surely show it
If you're happy and you know it,
Do all three.
(Clap hands, stomp feet, and nod head)

GREEN ● LIGHT

What makes your child happy? Ask your child and take a moment to record his responses either by writing them down or taking a video. One day you'll look back at the simple and creative answers and be glad you took the time to slow down and record this moment in time.

RESOURCES

HELPFUL RESOURCES

American Sign Language Web sites

Now that you've learned many ASL signs, why not test your knowledge and learn more by diving into some ASL Web sites? Hone your signing skills through puzzles and games that will help you learn while having fun!

www.apples4theteacher.com/asl

Want to get better at the American Manual Alphabet? Visit this site to print off American Manual Alphabet flashcards to use in the car, at home, or anywhere you have a quick minute.

www.aslpro.com/games

Visit this Web site to play Hangman, What am I?, Find a Match, and ASL Jeopardy. You'll also find a great online signing dictionary if you want to learn additional signs. This site also has a baby sign section dedicated to learning signs that you might use with your little one.

www.lifeprint.com/asl101

This is an excellent Web site for both ASL teachers and students. You will find not only free ASL lessons, but also many fun games including: practice quizzes, spelling quizzes, animated spelling quizzes, practice sheets, ASL word search, and more.

www.needsoutreach.org/pages/sl

If you are a teacher, this is a site for you. Learn specific signs for subjects such as biology, geography, elementary and secondary math, history, and more.

Baby Sign Language Web Resources

www.handspeak.com

This comprehensive Web site not only has a wealth of ASL information, but a special area dedicated to signing with your baby.

http://deafness.about.com/cs/signfeats1/a/babysigning.htm

Here learn the benefits of signing with your baby.

www.sign2me.com/

Want to enroll in a baby signing class or order additional materials related to baby signing? Visit this Web site to learn more.

www.babies-and-sign-language.com/

Web site dedicated to teaching parents about the benefits of using sign, FAQs, signs, and much more.

http://commtechlab.msu.edu/Sites/aslweb/browser.htm

Use this browser to discover signs for words you haven't yet learned.

References

Acredolo, Linda P., and Susan W. Goodwyn. "The Longterm Impact of Symbolic Gesturing During Infancy on IQ at Age 8." University of California, Davis & California State University, Stanislaus. Presented at the International Conference on Infant Studies, 2000.

Crais, Elizabeth R., Linda R. Watson, and Grace T. Baranek. "Use of Gesture Development in Profiling Children's Prelinguistic Communication Skills." The University of North Carolina, Chapel Hill, 2009.

Iverson, Jana M., and Susan Goldin-Meadow. "Research Report: Gesture Paves the Way for Language Development." The University of Pittsburgh & University of Chicago, 2005.

Trainor, L. J., and B. M. Heinmiller. "The development of evaluative responses to music: Infants prefer to listen to consonance over dissonance." *Infant Behavior & Development,* 21.

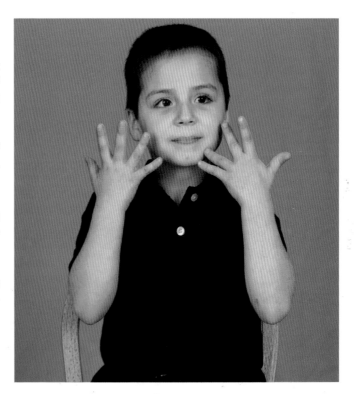

INDEX

INDEX

INDEX

INDEX

mL